STAGE *by* STAGE

STAGE *by* STAGE

75 YEARS OF THEATRE
IN MARKET HARBOROUGH

[signature: Matt Howling]

Henry Arthur Jones

updated by
Matt Howling

Matador
9 De Montfort Mews
Leicester LE1 7FW, UK
Tel: (+44) 116 255 9311 / 9312
Email: books@troubador.co.uk
Web: www.troubador.co.uk/matador

MARKET HARBOROUGH DRAMA SOCIETY
The Theatre, Church Square, Market Harborough, LE16 7NB

ISBN 978 1848760 738

Cover design by Alec Riddett and Rob Bartelt

Typeset in 10pt Palatino by Troubador Publishing Ltd, Leicester, UK
Printed in the UK by TJ International Ltd, Padstow, Cornwall, UK

Matador is an imprint of Troubador Publishing Ltd

To Alec and Marge
Who first landed me in this consomme

CONTENTS

ACKNOWLEDGEMENTS

The authors of this book would like to acknowledge everyone who contributed to it, especially the Market Harborough Drama Society and those members whose anecdotes and memories are included in its pages. Thanks must also go to Harborough District Council for its help in funding the book, society archivist Viv Window, and Rob Bartelt and Alec Riddett for the cover design.

DISTRICT OF
HARBOROUGH
RURAL SOUTH LEICESTERSHIRE

INTRODUCTION

For all its wonderful achievements, both on stage and off, Market Harborough Drama Society had something else to be proud of when it reached its 75th anniversary this year.

It was a milestone worthy of celebration – and some of the more pro-active members of the society got to work organising what form those celebrations should take. A number of events were planned. One aim was to update the book *Stage By Stage*, first published during the society's diamond jubilee year in 1993.

It was decided that, when the book was updated in the 75th anniversary year, the original *Stage By Stage*, conceived and written as a labour of love by the late Arthur Jones, who had long-standing links with the society, should remain intact. His efforts had produced a fascinating and valuable account of the society's colourful past, and it was agreed, his original text should not be altered.

Updating the book, however, would take just as much time and effort, as the last 15 years had seen many changes, as well as a number of memorable plays and performances. It would be a collaborative process. Many members of the drama society would contribute memories and stories to help fill its pages.

Though impossible to mention everyone who has contributed to the theatre and the drama society over the years, the aim of the new version of *Stage By Stage* was to promote and showcase what the society does, as well as capture and preserve, in writing, its important place within the town's history.

Matt Howling

PROLOGUE

This publication arose from the preparations for an exhibition of the history of the Harborough Theatre designed to celebrate the Diamond Jubilee of the Market Harborough Drama Society. Neither the exhibition nor the book could have been possible without the Society's superb archive to draw on. Contained in three massive scrap-books it preserves programmes, photographs and press cuttings of virtually every one of the Society's productions from the very beginning in 1933.

The collection was begun by Bert Webb, Theatre Manager and photographer who as a friend and neighbour of Harold Jones was able to assemble material from the early days and added steadily to it during his many years of service in the Society. The collection was then continued by Kathleen Plowman and by Lelia William-Kent, who carry it on to the present day. The Society owes a great debt to the three of them

Recourse has also been had to minute-books and newsletters and to long-standing members, whose recollections have added life to the written records. I am much indebted to them. But memory is a tricky thing and sometimes conflicting accounts emerge. Then I have had to guess at the most likely version and accept it. In all this, and in the task of selection from the mass of material available, I have been greatly helped by three wise guides, Freda Archer, Kathleen Plowman and Vivien Window, on whose judgement I have consistently relied. Where there are mistakes, however, they remain mine. In the selection and preparation of the illustrations the help of Alec Riddett and his colleagues at the Loughborough College of Art and Design is gratefully acknowledged.

The object has been to trace the life-story of the Drama Society as a collective body. Names inevitably occur but only where they illumine the general story: that has been the guiding principle. The effect will no doubt be to disappoint some readers who have been involved and who remember events or people differently. So to those who may be disappointed by what has been said and equally to those disappointed by what has been left out, I tender a comprehensive and sincere apology.

Arthur Jones

ACT 1 BEGINNERS (1933-44)

In 1570 Roger Ascham, who had been tutor to the young Elizabeth I, published an influential book on educational policy called *The Scholemaster*. In it he advocates the teaching of drama in school because it "gendereth good behaviour and audacitie". Throughout the reigns of Elizabeth, of James I and of Charles I there was much amateur drama by both children and adults – including James's Queen, Anne of Denmark, who loved dressing up and appearing on stage at court.

However, after the closure of all theatres by the Puritans in 1642, almost two centuries went by before amateur drama arose again; and then it was confined to a small section of the gentry, as when Dickens and his friends were at Rockingham Castle.

It was not until after the First World War that drama became a widespread leisure activity for the general public. It was fostered by the newly founded Women's Institutes and evening classes in drama sprang up in many places. In 1926 the Government issued a report, *Drama in Adult Education,* that emphasised the value of such classes, especially in rural areas and small towns. Already in 1919 the British Drama league had been founded by Geoffrey Whitworth to organise drama schools and festivals and to build up a library of plays, costumes and properties for local societies to borrow.

So in the early 1930s a small drama class was formed by the WEA in Market Harborough, meeting in the Old Grammar School, with a tutor from the Little Theatre in Leicester. In 1931 this was joined by Harold Jones, recently arrived in the town to take up a job with a firm of accountants. He found the class languishing and breathed new life into it. They moved to the Adult School at the corner of School Lane and Coventry Road. He talked them out of their idea of attempting to produce one-act plays. Instead he launched them into their first full-length production, *Candida,* which the programme describes mysteriously as "A Mystery in three acts by G Bernard Shaw". This was an ambitious undertaking by a new group and contrasts with the diet of light one-act plays favoured by WIs and other groups at the time. Harold Jones recalls with some hilarity his correspondence with Shaw over permission to do it. Blanche Patch, Shaw's secretary, sent one of the famous postcards saying that Mr Shaw would not give permission unless assured that the proceeds were not to be given to church spires or such other charities; he would expect, as with a professional production, a percentage of the takings. He was sent a postal order for 9s.2d!

The play was staged in the Recreation Club Room of Symingtons' corset factory on Thursday and Friday, 2-3 November 1933, and members of Messrs Symingtons' Orchestra were borrowed to provide musical items between the acts. Ella Sanderson, who played Candida, worked in Symingtons' office and through her influence no charge was made for the room, The programme however, listed only the characters and not the players: it simply concluded, "Produced, Stage-managed and Played by the Market Harborough Drama Class". That was the seed-bed from which the Harborough Theatre was to grow.

By the following November ambition ran even higher. The old Assembly Rooms in Abbey Street were hired – this time at £5 per night – for a production of Shakespeare's *Twelfth Night,* performed on Friday and Saturday evenings with a matinee on the Saturday afternoon. Harold Jones produced the play, devised and painted the scenery and played Sir Toby Belch; and rehearsals took place in his house. But there were evidently some casting problems. Photographs in the press show a predominantly youthful cast (some from the Grammar School no doubt). Looking through the cast list one notices a practice copied from hack professional companies but now mercifully abandoned: namely, resort to the Plinge family when the producer doesn't know who might be suborned to play a particular part. Here the Priest is down as Walter Plinge and the Dukes second officer as Samuel Plinge. Later on the Apothecary in *Romeo and Juliet* appears as Herbert Plinge. Happily that other such resource, Mr Weedon Owe, is absent.

The play was well dressed in Elizabethan costumes hired from Nathans, the players paying for the costumes themselves. Owing to a mix-up on the railway the hampers stood in Great Oxenden station for two weeks before the producer found where they were. By then it was the dress rehearsal and there was no time for fitting or adjustment. Nevertheless the press reports are highly favourable,

2

commenting particularly on the elocution. But there was a warning note: "Many people, most perhaps, were doubtful of its success, financial or otherwise. Events proved that they were quite wrong, for the Society (sic) did produce its play, not only successfully but brilliantly, and financially the results were not altogether discouraging". Part of the financial anxiety may have been that the Assembly Rooms were much larger than the factory club-room and a much bigger clientele had to be sought.

The problem recurs with the next production in the following March. The class had now been reconstituted as the Market Harborough Drama Society and the run was extended to three nights; but the press reported that "the house was not so large as desirable, but there were enough people there to show a full measure of enthusiasm" . The play was *Outward Bound*, a pseudo-philosophical piece about a miscellaneous collection of people in transition from this life to eternity, which had had some adverse criticism from churchmen when it first appeared in London. That Harborough audiences should regard it doubtfully was perhaps to be expected.

Nothing daunted, the Society offered Emlyn Williams's *The Late Christopher Bean* and *Romeo and Juliet* in the following season, 1935-36. New names appear as more mature players were drawn in to membership, players who figure regularly in leading roles over the years, such as Howard Biddlestone, Edward Lord, Isabel Peake, William C Wright who was also prominent in musical circles in the town, and P J Harris who was Maths master at the Grammar School.

Shaw's *Pygmalion* opened the 1936-37 season. This appears to have been only the second amateur production of the play in Britain. The cast list includes for the first time Kathleen Plowman, who had been a member of the class for some time and who was to prove the most durable, the most reliable and one of the most talented members throughout the life of the Society. She played Clara Eynsford-Hill. Eliza Doolittle was played by Hilda Dunkley who was said to be deeply embarrassed by the "Not bloody likely" line in front of her friends and family. (If this was still true in 1936, it reminds us how shocking that line would have been in 1913 when the play first appeared.)

Included in the programmes for this season was a leaflet which is quite revealing. It appealed for Patron Members who would pay an annual subscription "in return for preferential booking rights". The reason, it says rather plaintively, is that the Society "has spent over £100 per annum in production expenses since it started work". (Quite a slice of this had come from Harold Jones's own pocket.) Nevertheless the members affirm their belief that "the Drama can be a cultural force in the Town" and they will "continue producing…plays they consider worth while".

The response to this appeal is not recorded but the policy of selecting "worth-while" plays continued. In 1937 *Lady Precious Stream* was produced "according to the Chinese convention", in which one surviving member of the cast recalls acidly that no one had much idea what it was all about. Significant names that now appear for the first time include Joan Norman and Maurice Saunders.

Subsequent seasons brought out plays by Sean O'Casey, James Bridie and J M Synge, two Spanish imports by the Quintero Brothers and a Russian play by Kataev. In March 1939 T S Eliot's *Murder in the Cathedral* was performed in the Conservative Hall. It worried the reviewer in the *Mail* a good deal. His report begins by insisting that the play "is NOT a thriller" and he devotes several column inches to a balancing act between criticism of the choice of play and acknowledgement of the quality of performance. "The Harborough Society," he says "has frequently been criticised for its choice of plays . . . In these critical and anxious times a comedy will always attract a crowd . . . 'Murder in the Cathedral' would be described by some as depressing, certainly not a tonic for the jitters. . . In some quarters it is argued that it is the duty of the Society to consider its public when choosing plays. The question arises as to whether those who make this submission have seen the fine performances of the Harborough Society." He then points out that Bridie's comedy *Storm in a Teacup* drew in a larger audience at the Assembly Rooms than many of the other plays but goes on to praise the production and acting.

Matters were settled, for the time being, by the war. After a presentation of Shaw's *Misalliance* in February 1940 activities largely ceased for over four years. But, as will appear later, this issue of choice of play recurs over and over again in the life of the Society and at one point caused a serious rift. Contained within it are two conflicting factors. One is simply the budget. Unless sufficient seats are sold costs will not be met, and hiring costumes and wigs from a London costumier, as was the practice for the Shakespearean plays, is a very costly business. The other factor turns on quality. To build up a public for "worth-while" plays and educate its taste cannot be done with inept presentation. Whether the Society's policy of selecting plays of high literary merit was justified in these early years by the quality of performance is difficult to judge from the surviving records.

Almost all these productions were in the old Assembly Rooms in Abbey Street, now Edinburgh House. This was a large hall, opened in 1903 to replace the Corn Exchange as a venue for balls and public meetings and, in its early days, the Penny Popular Concerts and the Penny Readings whose proceeds helped to establish the Cottage Hospital. With its sizeable gallery it could seat some 500 people. But its platform was small and ill-equipped for drama. Two surviving photographs of the 1936 *Pygmalion* reveal a stage fairly wide but only a few feet deep so that the characters cannot but stand in a straight line. Ingenious replacement of one flat by a narrow French door in the back wall and switching of furniture from one side of the stage to the other were all that could be managed in the way of scene changing, and a row of battered troughs containing footlights provided most of the lighting. In these circumstances plays like *Twelfth Night, Romeo and Juliet, Juno and the Paycock, Lady Precious Stream,* with their large casts, must have presented a daunting challenge to the producer.

Harold Jones, however, who produced most of these plays, was one who would enjoy such a challenge. He was brought up in Birmingham and as a youth frequented the Birmingham Repertory Theatre which, under Barry Jackson, was a leading centre of innovative and high quality drama. That was where Harold Jones's theatrical tastes were formed. The fact that the Birmingham Rep had grown from an amateur company, The Pilgrim Players, may have reinforced his aspirations later in Market Harborough. Certainly he was the driving force in choice of play and he devoted himself to his productions with energy, dedication and a persuasive tongue. This is quite evident even though modesty caused him to keep the producer's name out of programmes wherever he could. He built up a Society of highly competent players and clearly had the nucleus of an appreciative audience. One of his appeals for Patron Members claims: "We are confident that there is not another Society in England with similar resources which has a better record of worthwhile plays of varied appeal". That is a perfectly justified claim.

Among the resources referred to here must be the total membership. The longest cast list is in *Lady Precious Stream* with 32 players. Perhaps not all were regular members. Some of the recitals mentioned below have 28-30 contributors and it is reasonable to conclude that the membership may well have been in the region of 35-40. How many Patron Members there were is not known. But in terms of personnel the resources were quite limited for the ambitious programme that was undertaken, including building the proscenium and sets, staffing the auditorium and often providing live incidental music.

In addition to the formal productions there were some informal and social occasions. In 1937 there was a Dramatic Entertainment in the Conservative Hall, including a scene from *Hamlet* and Galsworthy's one-act *The Little Man*. Later in the same year a Dramatic Recital in the Assembly Rooms comprised 22 excerpts from various Shakespeare plays. And there appear to have been private poetry recitals from time to time in members' homes. The programme for one of these announces engagingly: "The Second Part of the programme will consist of a few stale eggs. The organisers. . . wish to make it quite clear that they are in no way responsible for anything that happens after the Interval."

During the war years there are no records of activity. There would be no full productions but it may well have been that the informal recitals continued. Theatre did not entirely die out. The Freechurch Youth Movement presented programmes of plays, mostly one-acters and sketches, in the Methodist Hall; and as the war ended they joined with the Cooperative Youth Club in charitable performances in aid of the Hospital or, in one instance, the District Nurse's Car. Some Drama Society members appear in the casts, as well as several who were later to become stalwarts of the Society.

Apart from these shows, however, and the cinema, there would be little else in the way of entertainment and the eagerness with which the Society came to life again as the war neared its end suggests that the threads had been held together somehow behind the scenes. So the war brought down the curtain on an impressive First Act.

ACT II LODGERS (1944-62)

In July 1944 the Drama Society came publicly to life again with *The Importance of Being Earnest* performed at the Cooperative Hall. The press said, "There were obviously many people who last week made themselves acquainted with the work of the local players for the first time. . . Expressions of genuine surprise were heard at the polish and style attained by these amateur players." Five of the nine in the cast had been members in pre-war days, as had the producer, Harold Jones. A fresh experience, however, was that the house was full for all three performances, which augured well for the Society's future.

Contributing to the polish and style were the costumes, warmly commended by the reviewer. The men's costumes came from Nathan in London but the women's were designed and made by Joan Norman, who also played Cicely Cardew. This was to become a frequent feature of the Society's work in future years. Joan's husband, Bertie, who produced the scenery for almost all productions from the 1930s until the late 1960s, was a designer at Symingtons and could obtain remnants of appropriate materials which he and Joan then made up. During the war, however – and this may well have included *The Importance of Being Earnest* – they managed to get hold of a coffin-lining material, not from Symingtons, and used that successfully. It was treasure in those austere days.

Later in the year Harold Jones produced *Dangerous Corner* by J B Priestley, also at the Cooperative Hall; and early in 1943 another Priestley play, *When We Are Married.* Both productions had packed houses and although the stage was small ("They have had to perform," said a reviewer, and still have to do so in a room and under conditions not at all adequate") photographs show well dressed sets for both plays, though that for *Earnest* was described as "of wartime simplicity". However, concern about the choice of play re-surfaces. The Society, a reviewer writes, "have had some ups and downs in their career. They have had some successes and some, if not exactly failures, productions which appeared to arouse no enthusiasm on the part of the local public." Theatre critics everywhere are liable to display their independence by damning with faint praise, and players are wise to allow for this in their reactions. But the constant dripping of such reservations can influence decisions and it is clear from the productions of the next couple of years that tensions were arising in the Society.

From its inception the Society had been firmly under the direction of Harold Jones and hence was committed to a policy of presenting "worth-while" plays. In the first two years of the post-war revival this policy can be seen continuing: Wilde and Priestley have suitable literary standing (and drew the crowds). Then comes *A Murder Has Been Arranged,* which sounds more populist. But it was by Emlyn Williams, who had been included in the pre-war repertory, and it was produced by William Pratten, with Harold Jones merely stage-managing. This is not just a murder, but a ghost-story, and credit for suitable gruesomeness with green lights goes to Bert Webb on his first work with the Society. William Pratten, like several others who appear in cast-lists at this time, was a teacher in a school evacuated to the town. They were invaluable.

Next, in a move towards popularity, comes *The Magistrate,* a farce by Pinero produced again by Harold Jones. A notable newcomer to the cast is O de Rousset Hall, a future producer, Chairman, President and long-standing pillar of the Society. (And, alas, there is our old friend Walter Plinge again). It was given in Symingtons' Club Room and it has all the characteristics of productions of this period: excellent costumes, a tiny stage that forces players to stand in a line and play straight out to the front, a curtain set with one or two pieces of furniture of which the only practicable item is a settee across the middle, footlights, and awkward flies that make the top lighting patchy. There must have been much frustration for cast and stage management in coping with such disadvantages in a farce that requires a slick pace and four changes of scene. But the play seems to have been well received.

For the next two seasons the venue generally alternates between Symingtons and the Coop Hall, where facilities were even poorer. But after *The Magistrate* Harold Jones disappears from the scene (taking the available scenery with him). Where he got to will appear later. The immediate consequence is the emergence of a new generation of producers and a wider choice of play. Margaret Gray produces *Blithe Spirit;* T W Vernon produces *Maria Marten* "in the traditional acting version", in which Mervyn May and Rita Woodward first appear; and Joan Norman's long and distinguished career as producer begins with Martin Vane's *The Two Mrs Carrolls,* in which John Bunten, another future Chairman of the Society, comes out. That was in 1947.

A further milestone registered by this last play is the choice of the Conservative Hall which, in its various guises, was to remain the Society's home almost without interruption to the present day. It had already been used in the 1930s, for example with the much criticised production of *Murder in the Cathedral.* At that time the stage – platform would be a truer term – was only nine inches high, which was one reason for their preferring the Assembly Rooms. Now, however, the Society decided, partly for financial reasons and partly because the Assembly Rooms were showing signs of age, that they could make something of this small social club. The first move was to increase the height of the platform by building an upper stage on top of it. At the same time the front of the stage was edged forward to give a valuable bit of extra depth, though the acting area and the backstage space remained barely adequate.

Nevertheless the programmes for the next few years show what can be done, by imagination and ingenuity, with limited means. From 1947/8 the number of productions rose to five every year, occasionally with something extra, each running for three nights. The range of plays was widened to include some that were unashamedly popular, like *Ladies in Retirement,* in which John Moore, first of a notable family in the Society, made his debut. But in 1947/8 A A Milne, J B Priestley, Noel Coward and James Bridie appear on the bills; in the next season Priestley again, Dorothy Sayers and Somerset Maugham; in 1949/50 a version of *Alice in Wonderland* and another Emlyn Williams; and on to 1952, Coward, Milne and Priestley all appear again, with Rattigan, Eleanor Farjeon and of course Shakespeare. The post-war Society could not be accused of neglecting "worth-while" plays.

In this respect, however, they were now faced with competition. Harold Jones, having abandoned them in 1946, set up a rival company, the Apollo Players, "filled (he said) with the hope to find a small audience for poetry in the theatre". In the next seven years Apollo put on a series of classic plays, mostly in verse, that moved one reviewer to say: "Market Harborough playgoers have come to look for some brave ventures to the Apollo Players. They do not always approve of the ventures when they see them on the stage, it is true, but they do respect the courage of Mr Harold Jones and his associates in choosing the kind of plays which amateurs do not commonly risk." What plays ? Well, Sophocles' *Antigone* for one; a couple of 13th-century Chinese plays; *Gruach,* a blank-verse excursion into the early life of Macbeth; and Norman Nicholson's *Old Man* of *the Mountains,* the story of Elijah set in modern Cumbria, which caused outrage to some of the chapel-goers who attended the performance in the Jubilee Hall in aid of their repair fund. For a number of the early Apollo performances the audience was provided by German prisoners-of-war from the camp in Farndon Road; an officer acted as interpreter, explaining the action from time to time.

To have two lively societies like Apollo and the Drama Society complementing each other might seem a boon for, as one newspaper said, "We have more dramatic societies than you would expect to find in a town of ten thousand and . . . the members are keen – and more than usually talented". However, the fact is that to a large extent the two groups were drawing on the same pool of talent. The Apollo programmes do not give players names but in the press reports one recognises a number of familiar figures, some of whom must have been rehearsing simultaneously for the two societies. Indeed one MHDS producer of the time recalls with some bitterness the way his rehearsal schedule was "messed about" by the demands of Apollo.

This however was not true of everyone. One of the regular and most talented members of the Apollo Players was Betty Coles, who had graduated via the wartime youth groups. Then in 1950 she crossed the floor to the Drama Society to play in *To Kill A Cat,* and thereafter remained a faithful member to the present day, along with her new husband Bob Whitelaw. Later these two formed the Harmeth Players but never broke their connection with the Drama Society. Another newcomer at this time was Freda Hall (nee Clay), a regular for the next score of years.

This period saw some significant innovations. The 1950

production of *Alice in Wonderland* was the first Christmas play for children and was followed next year by *Toad of Toad Hall*, so beginning a long and still lively tradition. In September 1950 a production of Coward's *Private Lives* formed the centre-piece of the towns week-long celebration of The Battle of Britain; and that season ended with *A Midsummer Night's Dream* as a local contribution to the 1951 Festival of Britain. It also saw the first appearance of Cliff Hudson, later an inimitable Broker's Man in pantomime, and Gwen Ordish, another product of the youth groups, who soon became Mrs Hudson.

Photographs from this period reveal a progressive change. It is pretty clear that Harold Jones as a producer had been interested mainly in the script and the effective speaking of it, and relied on hired costumes for visual impact. His sets were simple, often merely curtains, and did little to establish an ambience for the play. Now that changes. Bertie Norman was a master of scene design and especially of painting and some of his sets for the exiguous stage of the Conservative Hall are astonishing for their combination of realism and practicality. He never drew a cartoon or made a model of a set, only a floor plan of flats, doors, windows, etc., but he clearly carried in his head a profound feeling for the setting of a play and could visualise it readily as a stage set. Fortunate indeed is the company that can call on such a gift.

There is great variety in his sets, from the half-timbered cosiness of the country house in *Busman's Honeymoon,* the cool baronial dignity of *She Passed Through Lorraine,* or the mannered Thirties' style of *Private Lives* to the exuberance of wings and backcloths for *Alice* or the *Dream.* These effects are all the more remarkable in that the scenes had to be erected and painted on the hall stage immediately before the dress rehearsal, as is the case for most societies lodging in other peoples premises. Then in 1952 a surprising new development suddenly made life easier all round.

Through the generosity of the proprietor of Webbs' Outfitters in Church Street, the Society was accorded the free use of a building behind the shop. This had been No 1 Aldwinckle's Yard in the days when much of Harborough had comprised narrow yards of densely populated cottages but, like all the rest of the yard, was now uninhabited. It had two floors, with an open staircase and a small side room on the upper floor, but there was no kitchen or even water supply, only a tap in the yard and an open drain. Domestic activity like making coffee and washing up meant encountering the elements outside.

This was christened the Club Room and for some 35 years it was an invaluable adjunct to the Society's activities. Whereas previously the Society was simply a collection of individuals who came together from time to time for a common project, the Club Room changed it into a genuine body with a base, a local habitation as well as a name. After some repair and decoration it was formally opened by Lewis Moore, the President, on 3 May 1952. Thereafter Friday night was Club Night when members gathered for informal socials, improvisations, sketches, play-readings, lectures, etc., with the Social Secretary, notably Joan de Rousset Hall, as hostess. It was something new and highly popular in the Society's life.

The great value of the Club Room however was that it afforded a rehearsal room and a scene-dock. The stage area at the Conservative Hall measured 12ft by 9ft, the size of a modest drawing-room carpet. It had therefore been quite feasible to rehearse in members' homes and the Eads's and the Halls' on Great Bowden Road, the Saunders's on Lubenham Hill, the Moores' on Bowden Ridge and the Normans' in Little Bowden had been regularly used so, though with some inconvenience to the families (especially, be it said, when TV sets appeared). Now the exact area could be marked out in the Club Room and rehearsals conducted as and when required. Moreover scenery could be set up and painted downstairs and a whole set assembled ready for transporting to the Hall for the dress rehearsal. A stock of steel-and-canvas stacking chairs was acquired for use not only in the Club Room but in the auditorium at the Hall as well. On the Sunday morning before a show a curious procession could be seen moving repeatedly along Church Street and behind the east end of the church: it consisted of two men some twelve feet apart, linked together by a long bamboo pole from which were festooned a dozen or so of these chairs which clattered together towards the middle as the pole sagged under the weight. They were followed by others bearing miscellaneous burdens of flats, furniture, lamps, dimmers, drums of cable and so on, And next Sunday they processed back again, seven or eight times each way. Mercifully, after a while Noel Dyson provided a truck.

The Society grew in strength and reputation in these years of the 1950s. Richard Thorndike, nephew of Dame Sybil and a reporter on the Harborough Mail, had joined in 1950, as had H L Moore, soon to be President. The whole Moore family were active in the Society and their home at White Lodge was the scene of much social activity. The Tugwell family followed: first son Julian; then Arthur, later to be Chairman and then President of the Society, played Bottom in the 1951 *Midsummer Nights Dream;* and Ethel's twenty-year service as producer began with *Cranford* in 1954 in which she also played the narrator Mrs Gaskell. Rita Woodward, who had been a prominent member from 1947, now brought in her husband Jack because, she said, he was tired of sitting at home waiting for her. He proved to have a comic talent that brought him a regular succession of parts. David Neal, the Society's most distinguished contribution to the professional stage, came out in *Our Town* in 1953. Percy Davey, later secretary to the Society, and Alan Archer were in the 1953 *Merchant of Venice;* and Freda Archer, who in the next forty years was to occupy almost every office in the Society – actress, producer, Treasurer, Chairman, Publicity and Bookings Officer, and friend to everyone came out as Gwendolen in *The Importance of Being Earnest* also in 1953. Ken Hankins, editor of the Harborough Mail and a notable player in comedy, joined in 1954/5 to appear in *Maiden Ladies;* and Gerald Heighton came in in the same season to play Touchstone in *As You Like It* (a production in which the Forest of Arden was graced with a tree of quite bizarre obscenity).

1957/8 season opened with Joan Norman's *Macbeth* in which Alec Riddett appeared for the first time, as the First Murderer. More importantly he helped Bertie Norman with the scenery, as he was to do for the rest of Bertie's life, later taking over as Artistic Director. Alec's immense contribution will become clearer later in the story but already in this first show his talents as both performer and painter were apparent. Other notable recruits at this time were Bryan and Betty Southwell; but in 1960 the Society lost David Neal to RADA and his impressive professional life.

In 1960 Harborough Construction (Harbilt) took over the lease of the Conservative Hall as their social club. It was re-named Liberty Hall by Symingtons, who still retained the ground floor as cycle shed and garage. The Society continued to hire the hall as before and were able to make some minor improvements. For instance the

Leicester Opera House stage curtains were bought at auction as the Opera House closed, and provided not only front curtains for the stage also light-proof drapes for the side windows of the Hall which had hitherto been a distraction, especially on light evenings.

The camaraderie of the Club Room engendered a good deal of the public spirit as well as helping with the formal productions. Already in November 1952 the production of *Bonaventure* was taken to Leicester, to perform in Messrs Hart & Levy's factory, through the influence of the President, H L Moore. Out of the Club Night improvisations there evolved a concert party that visited hospitals, to old people's homes and village halls for one-night stands. For World Refugee Year in 1960 the Society joined enthusiastically in the town's the fund-raising effort. As well as donating the proceeds – £50 – of Cliff Hudson's production of *Sailor Beware*, a "Black-and-White-Minstrel Show" (you could do such a thing in those days) toured the town on the eve of an Old-Time Market and raised another £20. And a float was regularly contributed to the town's annual Carnival.

Then in the following season, 1961/2, which opened with *Wild Goose Chase,* there was a special preview to which senior members of the District Councils were invited. The Urban District representation was led by the Chairman, Arthur Tugwell, as well known on the Harborough stage as in the council chamber; and the Rural District by its Chairman, Miss Saunders Morrison. They were welcomed from the stage by the Society Chairman, O de Rousset Hall, who was also the producer and who became Chairman of the UDC himself soon after.

This cultivation of outside contacts continued with a production of *Breath of Spring,* a zany farce directed by Kathleen Plowman and Alec Riddett and performed at St Nicholas Hall in Little Bowden. This was to celebrate the opening of the new hall for which the decoration had been designed by Alec. The Leicester Mercury reported that "facilities for both actors and audience are a great improvement on the Liberty Hall. . .and gave more scope for movement and improved scenery. The set created by Bert Norman and Alec Riddett was a masterpiece – one of the best amateur play sets I have ever seen." A newcomer to the cast was Richard Hill who later managed the Theatre's sound equipment for many years.

Looking back over these 18 years and more than 80 productions one is struck first of all by the range of plays selected: *The Merchant of Venice, A Midsummer Night's Dream, As You Like It, Macbeth, The Taming of The Shrew* and *The Tempest; The Importance of Being Earnest,* Anouilh's *Antigone. Under Milk Wood;* a regular series of lively farces from *The Happiest Days of Your Life* and *Wild Goose Chase* to *Doctor In The House;* some excellent thrillers like *Rope, Gaslight* and *Dial M For Murder.* The tradition of Christmas shows, begun with *Alice* and *Toad,* continued with a number of imaginative choices like Nicholas Gray's *Beauty and the Beast* and *Cradle of Willow, a* moving version of a Nativity play, and later, *The Holly and the Ivy.* These formed an alternation of children's and adults' Christmas plays well suited to the small stage and the Harborough audiences.

In most seasons there was a balanced list of five plays of different styles, all the more surprising in that there was no productions committee: it was left to individual producers to select plays pretty freely. Within this freedom however there was a tendency for regular producers to specialise – Joan Norman with Shakespeare and other classics; O de Rousset Hall with light comedy and farce (he later turned to pantomime); Ethel Tugwell with emotional drama; Ken Hankins with thrillers.

The rising quality of the sets has already been described. Lighting too improved as the Society acquired more equipment, though the low ceiling over the stage made hanging the lamps difficult and for a long time the old footlights were still in use. There was little room backstage for a control panel, only a couple of portable sliding dimmers that could be stored in the Club Room, and for every show cables had to be strung along the auditorium to bring power for the lighting board and the lights. Until 1957 George Brawn, whose electrical shop was in Coventry Road, was in charge, with a lot of uncredited help from Bert Webb; George was a law to himself, to be approached by producers with diplomatic delicacy. He was succeeded by Noel Dyson, manager of the area Electricity Board offices, who had already given invaluable help in all sorts of backstage operations and was a great servant of the Society.

In the press notices there are many tributes to excellent character performances, but there are also rather more compliments to the prompter than one would wish, as well as regretful comments on the occasional fluffed line and the evidences of under-rehearsal. Which leads to another striking feature, namely casting. Auditions were rare. Producers selected their casts as they chose. Many of the plays have very large casts and, despite the newcomers listed above, the acting resources of the Society remained quite limited. There was pressure on players to appear in several plays in succession, which was good for their experience: one is drawn to admire the versatility of many long-standing members. But much depended on the discipline that the producer could impose; and the Society's evident success throughout this period derived from a generation of producers who could cope with the physical limitations of the stage and exact committed team-work from their casts. That the occasional fluff was noticed is the best testimony to the general standard.

Press reviews also drew attention, rightly, to lapses of stage management ("It really is most infra-dig to drink brandy from cocktail glasses") but they fail to remark those triumphs of illusion that stage-managers have to achieve – like the rocking boat at the opening of *The Tempest* that made one of the extras sea-sick. Or, in one of the thrillers a victim is stabbed in the back by a pair of scissors: it was fashioned by Marjorie Riddett out of rubber with a short nail protruding from the end, which was plunged into a pad of foam rubber worn by the victim under his coat and stuck out with grisly realism as he fell forward. The aim had to be accurate: there was no understudy. As was said by the reviewer quoted above, "Small details are even more important when playing on a small stage"; but the most effective are those that pass unnoticed.

Details such as this underline the problems of production on a tiny stage in a hired hall. During the Harbilt tenancy of Liberty Hall these problems became worse as the company made more regular use of their social club and access by the Drama Society became more difficult to plan ahead. The production of *Breath of Spring* at Little Bowden enjoyed so much better facilities that the programme expressed the hope of further visits there. But they never happened, for by the next season a complete change in the Society's fortunes had brought an end to lodging in other people's halls.

ACT III TENANTS (1962-70)

On 6 September 1962 the Harborough Mail carried a somewhat breathless column about "the debut of the Harborough Theatre". "In recent weeks,' it said, "working parties of members and friends of the society have been busy in the hall with buckets, pails, mops and brushes, preparing the walls, etc., for the new colour scheme planned by the designers, Mr Bert Norman and Mr Alec Riddett."

The cause of all this activity was the Society's acquisition of the lease of the old Conservative/Liberty Hall. The reason for the withdrawal of Harbilt and the terms of the new tenancy are not recorded but the offer of the lease to the Society by R & W H Symington was due to the interest of James Hobbs, secretary to the company and a firm supporter of the Drama Society. He is reputed to have enjoyed being allowed a walk-on part whenever possible, preferably with no lines to speak.

Not only did this development bring to an end the problems of access that had arisen, but it fulfilled the long-held ambition of some older members to have a theatre of their own. So one of the first steps was to announce the change publicly by erecting a board with the legend HARBOROUGH THEATRE over the front door. It was a proud moment, intensified soon afterwards when Ralph Thurston, the noted local artist, produced the Harlequin sculpture that graces the Theatre front.

The season started with a special performance of *The Sound of Murder*, produced by Ken Hankins, before an invited audience. The official opening was performed by Lionel Hamilton, director of the Northampton Repertory Company. After congratulating the Society on its enterprise he urged everyone professional or amateur, "to strive to 'sell' the theatre to the man in the street and not regard it as an elect and select assembly for their own ends"; thus unwittingly raising memories of those old quarrels about choice of play. However, the chairman, O de Rousset Hall, with tactful ambiguity, announced, "We are determined to try to provide the very best in amateur theatre for the town"; and Marjorie Riddett's specially decorated cake was consumed on stage by the assembled

17

guests. Alas, Lionel Hamilton didn't get any, for it turned out that he was in the play at Northampton that night, though not on until the third act, which allowed him just time to do the honours and flee.

The tenancy related, of course, only to the upstairs room: Symingtons still used the ground flour as a garage and cycle shed. And this upstairs room was of a kind almost unimaginable to anyone who sees the Theatre now. In a corner at the back of the auditorium was small kitchen, the only place where interval coffee could be brewed. The auditorium had a flat floor, which meant that, except for the front row, actors were visible only from the waist up, so that anyone put to death disappeared from view before mortality was complete. (How Garrick would have fretted! He revelled in his death-scenes and changed the end of *Romeo and Juliet* so that he could die on the forestage and not in the tomb.) The flat floor had advantages, however: the hall was hired regularly by a dancing school and a Scottish Dancing group, which helped with the rent.

Then the stage: not only was it small – 12 ft by 9 ft – but down the right-hand side was a corridor leading to the one WC. Anyone paying an emergency visit during a performance was enjoined not to pull the chain. Backstage was a small dressing-room, very small and not well lit, and there was just space for a small props table Access to the stage, for which only one entrance was possible, was by a couple of wooden steps under which the sound-equipment was tucked a way. If the effects man had to operate this while an entrance was to be made, the actor had either to step on him or leap over his back.

This was the "theatre" about whose acquisition there had been so much excitement. But the excitement was justified. They had coped with these limitations for almost thirty years. In any case, ever since the Middle Ages there has been more drama done in inadequate fit-ups than in all the grand theatres put together. Now, just as the Club Room changed the character of the Drama Society, so their own theatre carried the change further. One deeply committed member recalls the thrill of pride she used to feel at seeing "Harborough Theatre" on the wall whenever she crossed Church Square.

Because the place was held on only a short lease there wasn't much that could be done in the way of improvements, other than redecoration. That in itself made a difference: the place began to feel more like a theatre and less like a hall. One major improvement was the creation of the Jam Shelf, an attic room tucked up in the roof over the kitchen at the back of the auditorium, to house the lighting and sound-equipment. Its sole means of entry was up the iron ladder that is still to be seen clinging to the wall on the first landing. The front being of glass, the operators had a full view of the stage, a huge benefit (though the single layer of glass allowed conversations within – not always complimentary to the performance – to be heard by half the audience). The consequent removal of the equipment increased the back-stage space, and the cables along the length of the hall could now be installed permanently and tidily.

The great advantage of the tenancy, however, was that sets could now be built on the stage and it was soon found that rehearsals benefited from taking place there and in the set itself. Gradually the Club Room came to be used as a store, particularly for costumes, so that a good wardrobe was quickly built up. But the Club Nights, which had been so popular and so influential in the life of the Society, began to lose their appeal.

The decision to take up the lease had not been arrived at lightly. Over the summer of 1962 there was much debate, especially about the financial commitment involved. Hitherto almost the only source of income had been ticket sales for shows. The cancellation of a show, an ever present possibility through sudden illness or accident (though it has happened only twice during the Society's history), would not mean much of a loss. Now, with the overheads, it could be serious.

Two factors thus combined to concentrate attention on the programme of plays: the exciting possibilities of the new Theatre and the need to maximise income. At the AGM of 1962 it was proposed that there should be a play a month: rehearsals could overlap by using the Club Room and the stage. Whilst this ambition was not quite realised, the 1962/3 season comprised seven full plays, plus a revue, *Nuts in July*, staged jointly with the Operatic Society in aid of a number of local charities; and there was also a visit by the Sibbertoft Players with their *Holiday for Simon*, offered as a contribution to Harborough Theatre funds. Most of the shows ran for four nights instead of the previous three.

The season included a notable production of Pinter's The *Caretaker* with a set that Alec Riddett regarded as the best he ever did. The three performances by Ken Hankins, Robert Whitelaw and Jack Woodward drew warmly favourable notices in the press; and the whole season was a great success with full houses and appreciative audiences. It might not have been possible without the arrival of some talented newcomers: Jean and Ian Joule, Janet Holyland (a former Apollo player), Jane Kirby, John White, Geoffrey Tomlinson (a monumental Hercules in *The Rape of the Belt*), and Muriel Lyon all joined at this time, presumably drawn by the dignity of a proper Theatre and the public attention focused on it.

The next few years saw similarly ambitious programmes. The seven plays of 1963/4 included *The Lady's Not for Burning, Othello* and *Look Back in Anger*. In 1964/5 there were again seven plays, including *Blithe Spirit, a* double bill of *Hamlet* and *A Midsummer Night's Dream* running on alternate nights over two weeks, with Roy Brown as Hamlet, and *September Tide* in which Bev Willis appeared for the first time. He and Roy Brown (Roy Macready) are two more of the Society's gifts to the professional stage. In 1965/6 there were *Must Fall* (with Norman Ward among the backstage credits), *Post-Horn Gallop,* directed by O de Rousset Hall and announced as the 100th post-war production, and a beautifully costumed *Ideal Husband;* and in the 1966/7 programme beside *Pygmalion* and *Murder on the Nile,* there was the first traditional Christmas pantomime, *Cinderella,* devised and produced by O de Rousset Hall, in which Pauline and Tony Moore joined the company as Dandini and an Ugly Sister respectively.

By this time the number of productions had dropped to six per year, partly because of the intensive use of the building. There were more visits by outside groups, such as the Carl Clifford Puppet Theatre from Northampton – there had been a surge of interest in puppetry during the previous few years, because of the growing demand for puppet shows on TV. But more particularly the Club Room was proving unattractive as compared with the Theatre. It was cold, it had no, toilet, it had no kitchen and it was showing signs of wear. Some training evenings were held there in 1964, when Jean Joule did Voice Production and Movement in Costume. But soon afterwards the Club Nights were transferred to the Theatre as Friday Socials. The stage was more attractive for rehearsal too and the idea of overlapping, with rehearsal starting in the Club Room and then transferring to the stage when the previous play was over, proved unappealing. Comfort will always seduce people from stoic duty.

Despite the evident success of the productions, then, tensions were again arising, though not this time about the choice of plays, for a loyal clientele was being built up that would support the broad range that was being offered, from classics to thrillers to farces. It was rather that sustaining these intensive seasons focused attention on the physical limitations of the place. Frustration was being felt by players and by producers, but most of all by the technical crews. A player might appear in two or even three plays in a season; some producers might work on two; but the scene-builders and lighting crews were engaged on every one and their access was being limited by the constant use of the building for other purposes. Soon, Sunday mornings were the only time they could claim.

From all sides therefore came pressure for improvement and already in 1964 the establishment of a Theatre Improvement Fund was mooted. It could not be much more than a gesture for the whole future of the Theatre was uncertain. The lease was a short one; R & W H Symington had been taken over by Courtaulds and no one knew what might be the consequences; and the factory employees were no longer using bicycles. If the factory no longer needed the ground floor, what would be the attitude of the parent company?

Boldness often creates its own luck, and this was the case here. Symingtons offered the Society an option to purchase the building. What an opportunity! But of course there were misgivings about the funding. However, it was decided to launch an appeal for £10,000 which would meet the cost of some needed improvements as well as the purchase price. Two groups were set up: a national appeal chaired by Leslie Cockerill and a local fund-raising committee chaired first by Ian Joule and then by Jim Henderson. That was in May 1968. By December the fund had reached £1600 after a half-year of energetic organisation of fetes, dances, coffee mornings, sponsored walks and the like. The Urban District Council were unable to make a grant at this time but as an alternative offered a plot of land on The Commons, at a rent of a shilling a year, for the building of a new theatre. Calculation of the cost however, some £25,000 for the kind of building required, ruled out that option. In any case there was great popular attachment to the old Theatre, despite its shortcomings.

This was where the luck came in. Sir Frank (later Lord) Kearton, chair of Courtaulds, following an approach from Mr (later Sir) John Farr, MP, fixed a purchase price of £7,000 and granted an interest-free loan of the whole amount for five years, to allow time for the money to be raised. It was an act of heart-warming generosity and gave an immense boost to the fund-raising effort.

The national appeal had gathered support too – for instance, a letter of support from Prince Philip and donations from a number of theatre personalities including Dame Edith Evans. Local efforts proceeded vigorously, the most durable of these being the weekly coffee-mornings on Tuesdays and Fridays – market days – set up by Ethel Tugwell and Mary Webb and still raising a useful income to the present day Week by week the local press carried lists of donations from well-wishers and the proceeds of innumerable initiatives such as the collecting tins in fifty shops, pubs and clubs. The generosity of Courtaulds was matched by the generosity of the town.

Meanwhile the shows must go on and here too the excitement of the time is evident. The 1967/8 season included Anouilhs *Waltz of the Toreadors,* described by the press as "a difficult play for any company, for its mood varies so rapidly from comedy to high drama and then to pathos, with a touch of fantasy", all of which the production realised successfully. Contributing to its success was a first appearance by Sheila Dean. This ambitious season continued with *Fools' Paradise,* which had one of those (fortunately rare) disasters when the leading lady went down with tonsillitis after the first night and the part had to be played by the prompter; then *The Winter's Tale* and finally an *Old Time Music Hall,* a serious attempt to re-create a typical bill of the year 1900, thanks to help from the vice-chairman of the British Music Hall Society who advised on the programme, provided many souvenirs for an exhibition that accompanied the show, and attended the first night himself. To be able to sustain a season with such large casts in the midst of relentless fund-raising is a great tribute to the acting members as also to the technical team of Alec Riddett as designer, Norman Ward for lighting, and Richard Hill for sound, which was established at this time and remained so for the next decade.

A high-light of the following season was an acclaimed production of Coward's *Private Lives* with another newcomer, John Taylor, and Jean Joule in the leading roles. That year there were only five plays but in 1969/70 steam was got up again with six full productions plus a revue, *Anything Can Happen*, given by the Society's Youth Theatre. To help with the fund-raising there were also a couple of variety shows by the Dance School and a very popular charity appearance by David Kossof.

So, on this high note, in April 1970, and with all the excitement of newly-weds with their first mortgage, the Drama Society took possession of its own Theatre.

Romeo and Juliet 1936
Assembly Rooms

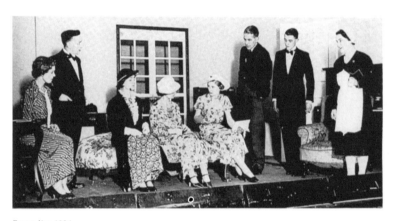

Pygmalion 1936
Assembly Rooms

Dangerous Corner 1944
Cooperative Hall

Ladies in Retirement 1944

Alice in Wonderland 1950

Merchant of Venice 1953

As You Like It 1955

A Midsummer Night's Dream 1951

The Importance of Being Earnest 1953

Cranford 1954

Dr Morelle 1959

Bonaventure 1953, Set by Bertie Norman

The Caretaker 1963

The Caretaker Set by Alec Riddett

The Club Room 1952

Erecting the Harlequin sculpture

The Theatre interior before reconstruction

The Heartless Princess 1973

Boeing, Boeing 1975

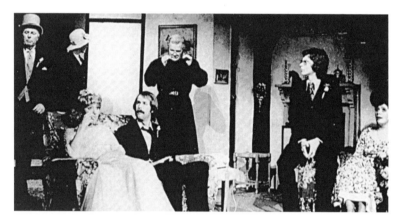

Halfway Up the Tree 1978

The Holly and the Ivy 1978

ACT IV OWNER – OCCUPIERS (1970-1979)

The building acquired by the Society, though soberly described in official records simply as No 14 Church Square, is one of the jewels in Market Harborough's architectural crown. Not only does it occupy a prime site, forming most of one side of the square and linking in with the red brick bow-front of the Symington factory, the warm stone of the parish church and the timber of the Old Grammar School to present a summary of the town's building styles, but it has its own story to tell.

The late J C Davies, the Harborough historian, quotes a tradition that the medieval presbytery, probably a timber building, stood on this site: the priest's door into the chancel is straight opposite. The earliest record of a building here is in one of the ancient deeds now framed and hanging on the walls of the Coffee Lounge. On 16 October 1672 Simon Buttriss, a grazier, sold to Thomas Lee, Gentleman of East Farndon, "all that cottage or tenement and its appurtenances" for £60, not a bad price. The tenant was Richard Barwell, a roper. Ten years later the price had risen to £185 but it now included a couple of cottages as well. Soon afterwards a "hovel" 7 yards wide by 3 yards was added to the property, with the garden of 21 ft by 14 ft adjoining, and the whole passed into the hands of the Clarke family who held it for over a century. It was now called or known by the name of The Green Dragon".

By the end of the 18th century the little garden was used as a Dunghill but the ancient tenement continued to include a public house, The Green Dragon, until 1908 when it became unoccupied. In 1924 it was sold to R & W H Symington, who then sold the little cottage next door for the Urban District Council to erect public conveniences. Later, in 1935, they pulled down the old pub to build a "Cycle store and room over".

This is the building that has been the scene of our story so far. Its unlikely frontage, of Northamptonshire ironstone with mullioned windows and Collyweston slate roof, is reputed to have been commissioned by Symingtons' managing director as his office window looked directly on to it and it would remind him of his home in Dingley – a touching thought. There was a further transformation during the Second World War when the ground floor was turned into an air-raid shelter. So altogether it was an interesting but pretty rum place that the Society was taking on. All the same, it deserves better than the dismissive sentence in Pevsner's latest Leicestershire volume of *The Buildings of England*: "No 14, a storehouse of 1935, surprisingly converted into a theatre".

What to do with it, now they'd got it ? There were so many things crying out to be done. As has already been shown the so-called theatre upstairs was seriously inadequate. The ground floor, whose space was so badly needed for so many purposes, was – and looked like – just a cycle-shed. And the appeal for £10,000, which would have allowed £3,000 for immediate improvements, was a long way short of its target.

Nevertheless, by April 1970 it was possible to put on an exhibition of models, plans and drawings of the proposed improvements. There would be two phases. First, the ground floor would be turned into a foyer and coffee lounge, with a kitchen at the front and a smaller rehearsal or committee room behind. At the same time, the auditorium upstairs was to have a face-lift, increasing the number of seats and raising the back rows on rostra to improve sight-lines. The second phase would include an external fire-escape (in place of the iron ladder down the wall), new toilets downstairs so that the stage could be widened, and a dressing-room and stage workshop also downstairs. New seating was to be secured by a "Give-a-Chair" scheme: anyone donating £4 would have his/her name inscribed on the back of a new moulded plastic chair. The exhibition, with John Ward the architect and Alec Riddett the designer in attendance, attracted a great deal of interest, as the press put it, "among the many organisations who will be taking the opportunity of using these fine facilities".

The whole project, designed to offer "excellent theatrical, social and cultural facilities for the town", took a long time to realise but it laid down the basis of developments over the next few years. What was clear, however, was that it would have to be very largely a do-it-yourself job. Local firms generously donated materials but the labour came once more from the energy and goodwill of the members. One member, Bill Kent, came forward with the offer of a thousand hours of work. His diary, which survives, lists the range of jobs he undertook and the hours spent on them – plastering, carpentry, painting, cleaning up, working on the toilets, the stairs and the kitchen. Then, as his thousandth hour ticked away he said with a grin, "Time's up", downed tools and went. Thanks to him and to many other members, the Coffee Bar was open for business by August 1970 – a remarkable achievement.

The old garage became the kitchen, a hatch and doorway were opened up and the whole of that wall was lined with pine boarding. The end wall and the ceiling were treated with silver tiles that helped to compensate for the lack of daylight. The front door leading directly into the Coffee Lounge was given an internal glazed porch to keep out draughts, and the other door at the foot of the stairs, which had hitherto been the theatre entrance, was retained for that purpose. The dividing wall between the staircase and the cycle-shed was opened up so that, already when the season opened with John van Druten's *Bell, Book and Candle,* the Coffee Lounge could be used as a foyer and for interval drinks. Even before that a series of Teach-ins had been started and the attractions of the Coffee Lounge were being enjoyed by the Youth Theatre and by Society socials.

One chore that was not killed off, however, was the carrying of chairs. For every show the new moulded-plastic chairs – still, incidentally, in daily use twenty-three years later – had to be carried up to the auditorium, clipped together in rows to satisfy the fire officer, carried down for Tuesday and Friday coffee mornings and back up again for the evening performances. A few years passed before more chairs could be afforded to save all this labour.

As yet not much could be done with the Theatre itself. However, progressively over the next couple of years some of the planned improvements took shape. In the area behind the Coffee Lounge men's and women's toilets were installed and a dressing-room, spacious by comparison with the old one, was created complete with mirrors and tables, racks and shelves for costumes, and good lighting. A new staircase led up to the backstage area which was enlarged by the removal of the old dressing-room and WC and enclosing a bit of flat roof.

What distinguishes a theatre from a hall is a proscenium. The old hall never had one. Because of the side corridor the stage was off centre and was framed in a very temporary fashion by the stage curtains from the old Opera House. Now however the corridor was removed, adding 3-4 feet to the width of the stage, and a solid-looking proscenium could be built. At the same time part of the backstage space was built up to stage level and added to the acting area, making it almost square where previously it had been wide and shallow. The effect was remarkable: audiences saw a true theatre when they came in; actors felt they had so much more space for movement; and producers had to re-think their techniques.

A critical part of the producer's job is "blocking" a play; that is, identifying the moves to be made by the players at specified speeches and designing the location, or grouping, of the players on the stage so that the audience's eyes will be drawn to the most significant character at a given moment and no player will be masking another from view, it is like the composition of a picture. The proscenium affords a frame for the picture. But this is a three-dimensional picture and the proportion of width to depth is more important than that of width to height. A shallow stage – as was seen so often in the early productions – offers little option but to have the players more or less in a line, with most moves made laterally across the stage.

In 18th-century theatres, with no lighting but two hoops of candles over the forestage, lateral movement was the norm and an upstage entrance was almost unknown. By the mid-19th century, despite greatly improved lighting, "crossing the stage" – a scissor movement of two actors passing each other – was a fixed ingredient of what came to be known as The Old School of acting (or "Ham"). It now looks impossibly artificial, though amateurs on a shallow stage are still tempted to do it. Press notices of the Society's productions in the 1950s and 1960s sometimes comment unfavourably on it.

Hence adding a few feet to the depth as well as to the width of the Harborough stage gave producers a new freedom that some, long used to the old conditions, had to learn to exploit. Freedom for actors too: more than one now discovered with glee the trick of "upstaging" a fellow-player, forcing him to turn away from the audience to respond. There are of course different ways of turning on a stage, depending on the manner in which the weight is transferred from the downstage to the upstage foot: a turn can itself convey eagerness, anger, resignation, fear and so on. A well-proportioned acting area enables ensemble playing of greater subtlety to spark that electric discharge between characters that makes a scene come vividly to life. So there turned out to be a happy congruence in the training sessions that were held, first in the Club Room and then in the Coffee Lounge, to prepare for the opportunities of the enlarged stage.

There was still a snag however. The main hall had a ridge roof running fore and aft along its length and tied together with steel rods (it couldn't help looking like a barn when the house lights were up), but the backstage area had a lean-to roof which was much lower. Now the rear extension to the stage had a ceiling that was only eight feet from the floor. Only eight-foot flats could be used all round the stage – as compared with the ten-foot flats now in use – and a rostrum of any size at the back of the stage would lift a tall player absurdly high. Moreover, lighting the rear stage was a constant problem.

This snag was encountered head on in the first production to use the enlarged stage, the 1971/72 pantomime *Jack and the Beanstalk*. The giant beanstalk rose realistically from the ground and disappeared above, ready for Jack, played by Jill Willis, to climb, When she reached the top there was no more headroom and she had to lie across the rafters until the end of the scene. Choosing that particular pantomime displayed the same brave refusal to be daunted by physical limitations as throughout the whole previous history.

Even before the stage was altered the programmes showed undiminished enterprise, for instance in *Tom Jones* with a cast of 21 and dramas such as *Spring and Port Wine* and *The Deep Blue Sea*. In 1970/71 there were six plays, plus another fund-raising revue in association with the Operatics and some Friday Socials that included a music-and-comedy evening and a 1920s film show called *Flashback*. The following season there were again six shows including the Peter Shaffer double bill *The Private Ear* and *The Public Eye*, an Agatha Christie, *The Chalk Garden*, and *The Chiltern Hundreds*. There was also an innovation in the visit of an amateur group from Manchester, The Tudor Players, to present *Say Who You Are* for a four-night run. This is a team that plays only away games, performing at drama festivals from Felixstowe to the Isle of Man. Their appearance in Harborough was due to two of their leading members, Ian and Queenie Parry, who had recently moved here and who were, as will appear, to become prominent members of the Harborough Society.

Other newcomers at this time included Janet and Andy Munro, Ben and Godfrey Tabiner, Margaret Chapman, Christine Staples, Barry Summers and Gordon Henderson; and in the set-building credits is the name of Wystan Baker who continued in that role for over a score of years, as well as becoming Theatre Manager and Licensee and later Trustee.

The fund-raising effort that had continued with unflagging energy and astonishing success was boosted by a grant of £200 from the Urban District Council and £50 from the Rural District and by sizeable donations from various individuals including Viscount Kemsley and Mr Lindsay Symington. At a General Meeting in December 1971 the Chairman, O de Rousset Hall, said: "Few would have believed three years ago when the Theatre Appeal Fund started that we could have achieved nearly £8,000 in such a short time." So further structural improvements could now be undertaken and the repayment of the purchase price could be foreseen.

For the 1972/73 season a change of policy was announced. There were to be only five productions, two before the Christmas show and two after. The reason given was to concentrate on quality. "Having made such good progress on the theatre itself," said the Chairman, we have got to consider seriously the use to which we put our theatre. Now we have got to concentrate on our productions – to fulfil our purpose in life, to offer the public a good programme of theatre as our contribution to the cultural life of the town." Maybe there was a certain weariness after the demands of the last three years. There was, however, enough energy to put in a raked floor along the length of the auditorium to improve sight-lines and an external fire-escape was installed by the end of 1973.

The concern for quality was being taken seriously. The Newsletter for November 1972 proposed that "Oscars" should be awarded for Best Production, Best Actor, Best Actress and Best Newcomer, and nominations were invited. Perhaps it was taken too seriously. There were only four productions that season, three of them by new producers. Barry Summers opened with *Oh What a Lovely War*, Queenie Parry produced *The Heartless Princess* for

34

Christmas and Andy Munro ended the season with *Sweeney Todd* for which the stage crew were very proud of their barber's chair, mounted on a rostrum and pivoted so that it could tip over backwards and decant the victim out of sight. But nothing more is heard of Oscars.

However, the next season, 1973/74, brought out six plays, again with a number of new producers – Ian Parry with *Pools Paradise,* Sheila Dean with *Summer of the Seventeenth Doll* and Gordon Henderson with the thriller *The Unexpected Guest.* In fact it was becoming clear that the Society had entered a new phase. There were newcomers to the acting strength, to the list of producers and to the backstage crew. At the same time a number of long-familiar names disappear from the programmes. It was as though, while the old core of members had been preoccupied with the appeal and the improvements, centre stage had been taken over by a new generation.

You cannot have a phoenix without a fire. It would be idle to pretend that the changes that overtook the Society in the later 1970s came about without tension. Several factors coincided to drive the process of change. One was simply the passage of years, charmingly known as natural wastage: people moved away, acquired other responsibilities, or found they could no longer perform as they had. Another was the influx of new members, many of whom had extensive experience elsewhere, including professional experience; they brought different perceptions of how the Society might run and were apt to be impatient of the old ways.

The most insistent engine of change, however, was simply the fact of owning property, for this, as many have found, concentrates the mind wonderfully. The euphoria of the appeal has already been described: it was a magnificent effort, involving a lot of people in a great variety of social and theatrical activities quite apart from the formal plays. The corporate life of the Society had never been so vital and so close. Behind the-absorbing busy-ness there had, of course, to be firm financial control. This was in the hands of a small and very competent band, notably Leslie Cockerill, Wystan Baker and O de Russet Hall. For most of the members this was all in the background: their concern was with the total sum to be raised.

Now, however, the dull business of finance came to the fore. Previously unknown matters like rates and tax had to be faced. On advice from the St Albans Theatre, which had already gone through a similar process, the first step was to register as a charity. After lengthy consultation with the Charity Commission this was secured, with a consequent reduction of rates and liability to tax. To achieve this status trustees had to be appointed and an acceptable constitution submitted. Nothing prolongs debate more mercilessly than the terms of a constitution; nothing so effectively provokes challenge to accepted ways of doing things. You cannot put into a constitution, "Decisions about any problem will be left to common sense in the light of circumstances at the time," which had been the way hitherto. So a prescriptive constitution came into being, with sub-committees for this and that – and Rules. Among others were Rules for Producers, importing ideas like casting by audition, a ban on producers appearing in their own plays and an attempt, largely ineffective, to require a budget for each production.

It was in this climate of change, creating a businesslike theatre management, that, almost by coincidence, changes of personnel took place. Bert Webb, who had joined the Society in 1945 and for thirty years had acted as theatre manager, performing all front-of-house duties, checking the safety, cleanliness and good order of the house with the constant help of his wife Mary, retired and was succeeded by Wystan Baker. Joan Norman, a member from 1937 and responsible for some of the most striking productions ever since, was forced by illness to give up producing after the 1975 *Hay Fever*. Ethel Tugwell, who had been producing regularly for over twenty years, concluded hers with *The Day After the Fair* in 1975. Arthur Tugwell, now President, gave his last stage performance in *Come Closer Now* in 1976; and long-established players like Ken Hankins, Rita and Jack Woodward, Cliff and Gwen Hudson, Freda Hall and others, had left the Society (though some of these reappear later in the story).

Their places were taken, as already indicated, by an influx of fresh talent. Newsletters, now a regular means of communication with a growing membership, appeal for people to come forward as producers and the idea of apprenticeship to an experienced producer is introduced. But the programmes at this time show a long list of new producers: Gordon Henderson, Sheila Dean, John Taylor, Doris Purnell, Ian and Queenie Parry, Jan Wilson, Bryan Southwell and, a little later, Ann Height. All of these also appear on the stage and the pool of players is further enlarged by such as Carole White, Tom Henderson, Beryl Taylor, John Burgess, Anne Hepworth, Vic Fyson, Susan Cooper, Diane Rickard and Eric Smith.

There was therefore no difficulty in maintaining the customary seasonal programmes. In 1975/76 the six shows include a lively *Salad Days* produced by Jean Joule, then Doris Purnell's *Plaza Suite,* described by a press report as being "about the comic goings-on in Room 719. But more than anything its about Ian and Queenie Parry. . .a real tour de force from the husband and wife team"; and an elegant *Lady Windermere's Fan.* The following season saw a total of eight shows, opening with *Alfie,* produced by John Taylor and Bryan Southwell and taxing the ingenuity of the stage crew with its rapid succession of scenes; then an evening of Dylan Thomas called *Come Closer Now,* hastily devised to replace an aborted production; Shaw's *Arms and the Man,* produced by Jan Wilson; another musical, *The Boy Friend,* with Gordon Birch and Rocky Knight in leading roles and remembered by many as one of the happiest productions; and Anouilh's *The Lark.* The season ended with another visit from the Tudor Players with their award-winning *Butterflies Are Free.*

Another departure in the 1977/78 season was a so-called Studio production. This arose from a recrudescence of the ancient debate (never entirely silenced) about "worth-while" plays. The Society's annual programmes had settled down to six, occasionally five, shows of a common pattern – dramas, thrillers, comedies, a Christmas play, with the occasional classic – almost always of well-known and established dramatists. A small group of members, led by Ann Height, pointed to a world of unusual, challenging, or experimental drama that was hardly explored. Fears that Harborough audiences would resist such adventures led to the idea of a Studio Production, additional to the regular season, done with minimal staging and minimal interruption of the regular rehearsal schedule. In the common English way, because Ann Height had proposed the idea, she was told to get on with it.

The result was a remarkable production of Sartre's *Huis Clos* on an apron put up in front of the closed stage curtain, described by a reviewer as "one of the most disturbing plays I have ever seen." The red stage curtains, lit only from front-of-house, gave an intense feeling of Hell, where the play is set, and the intimacy between apron-stage and audience worked powerfully, as was manifest in the open discussions that were arranged to follow the performance led by the producer, the cast and a visiting university lecturer. It was an auspicious innovation that might have set a trend but for the radical alterations that were soon to follow.

Membership of the Society continued to grow, as did public support. Plays now ran for five nights and were often sold out. The need for front-of-house staff – stewards, programme-sellers, coffee-makers – called for more involvement of non-acting members. The list of acting members also grew: Leslie Verrinder, Paul Roberts, Vivien and Alan Window, John Clarke, Fi Plowman, Diane Fox-Kirk, Phoebe Ravenhall, Jeanne Moore, and among producers, Nick Lewis and Arthur Jones emerge at this time.

Meanwhile the Social Committee led by Doris Purnell was valiantly arranging events of which some, like the major parties and some poetry evenings, especially those in members' homes, were very successful. For the Queen's Jubilee in 1977 an elaborate celebration included a Mystery Play on a cart in Church Square and a son-et-lumiere on the history of the town, to be staged against the Old Grammar School. Unfortunately, by sundown the townsfolk were in such a noisy state of patriotic euphoria that the tape couldn't be heard and the show was called off.

But the Society's style of life had changed, in parallel with social changes generally. The idea of an informal club night had little attraction and the occasional recitals and lectures, though appreciated, had relatively small attendances. Nor were there many visits from outside companies, though the Cine Society used the Theatre for their shows, as did the Natural History Society for their film evenings. The Coffee Lounge continued to be used by the Art Club and the Photographic Society for their annual exhibitions, and through the good offices of Wystan Baker the Sunday School from St Dionysius came in to use it on Sunday mornings.

As in the past the set-builders under Alec Riddett's direction, chiefly Eric Smith, Wystan Baker and Arthur Jones, strove constantly against the narrowness of the building. There was virtually no wing space; so the normal theatrical method of erecting flats with braces and stage-weights was unavailable. Every box-set became a major carpentry job with flats braced securely to the walls and battened together for rigidity. Changes of set were almost impossible even with front curtains closed. For pantomimes and such, old-fashioned wing-and-backcloth scenery had to be used, with cut-outs that could be hooked on to the wing-flats and an ingenious system of ropes and dog-leads that could turn the back-drop head over heels. The rear stage still had only eight feet of height and despite progressive acquisition of more equipment the problems of lighting remained serious. Nevertheless the quality of the scenery for all the plays was consistently commended, chiefly because of Alec's skill as designer and painter.

The 1979/80 season ended with a sumptuous revival of *The Importance of Being Earnest*, given in the original four-act version of 1894 and produced by Maggie Neal. A new feature was a gala charity performance, with supper, on the Monday, extending the run to six nights. But some continuity with the past was afforded by Kathleen Plowman who played Miss Prism as she had in the 1953 production. "It's funny," she said to the press after a rehearsal, "how you expect things to be just as you left them even after such a long time. . .I expect people to be in different places, and the entrances are the other way round."

On the old stage of 1953 entrances couldn't be any other way: there was only one (unless you hid out of sight on the blind side before the curtains opened and stayed trapped there until they closed again). So here is evidence of the improvements of the last twenty-five years. Now further improvement was imminent, for already a new appeal had been launched, with a much more ambitious scheme of development. When the curtain came down on *The Importance of Being Earnest* in May 1980 it came down on the stage which, as Conservative Hall, Liberty Hall and the first Harborough Theatre, had been the Society's home since 1947.

Ironically, it was at this very moment that the Department of the Environment decided to list 14 Church Square as a building of architectural and historical merit: which it undoubtedly is.

Ghosts 1975

*The Importance of Being Earnest
1980*

Lady Windermere's Fan 1976

Tartuffe 1979

40

O de Rousset

Ian Joule

Ann Height

Arthur Jones

Jill Perry

Jeanne Moore

Ian Parry

Freda Archer

Alec Riddett

Model of the rebuilt Theatre

The Coffee Lounge 1970

Hotel Paradiso 1980

The Conjur'd Spirit 1980

Oh What a Lovely War 1972

The Boy Friend 1976

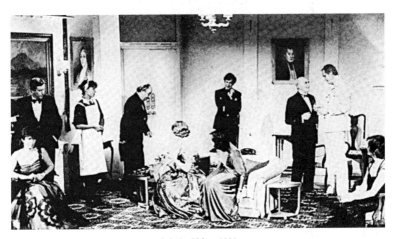

Relative Values 1984

Present Laughter 1984

43

The Gioconda Smile
1986

John Bass as King Rat,
Dick Whitttington 1985

Pack of Lies 1988

Round and Round the Garden 1980

She Stoops to Conquer 1988

44

ENTR'ACTE
BUILDERS (1979-1981)

All through the period since the Theatre was purchased improvements had been going on. Apart from the structural alterations other changes were made: a display window was installed at the front, gas central heating was put in, a permanent bar-counter was built in the Coffee Lounge, the seats were fitted with cushions made by members. But the old place was incapable of further real improvement as a theatre. Its awkward shape, long and narrow, tapering towards the rear so that the walls crowded in on the stage, and the lack of headroom over the stage were features from which there was no escape. These disadvantages the Society had surmounted for years; it could only expect to go on doing so.

Except, of course, that the leading figures in the Society now were relative newcomers and conversation turned often into speculation about how the Theatre could be enlarged. The urge towards enlargement was given added momentum by the threat of financial crisis. From 1976 there had been trading losses owing to falling ticket sales and the effects of inflation. The books had been balanced only by a large-scale Christmas Fair in 1977 and again in 1978 and by a profit of almost £500 on social events. Financial stability seemed to call for a larger building to produce a larger income.

The yard at the back was explored but the owners were unresponsive. There was a small garden alongside, but not available. A friendly architect produced a scheme to raise the roof but this would not have increased seating capacity. Hopes rose when it was rumoured that the Council were to demolish the public toilets next door and relocate them elsewhere; but the Council decided to refurbish them and leave them where they were.

It was at this point that there occurred three serendipitous conversations that altered the whole prospect. The first was between Alec Riddett, Artistic Director, and his neighbour Herbie Austin who was a director of one of the town's major building firms. Out of this emerged the idea of extending the first floor, since the ground floor could not be enlarged, by cantilevering out over the public toilets. Sketches on the back of an envelope showed this to be quite practicable but at a cost of at least £50,000. End of that idea.

Next the Chairman found himself chatting to a former colleague who had changed career and become a professional fund-raiser. Although the latter didn't know Harborough well and had visited the Theatre only once he gave it as his immediate opinion that such a sum could be raised without difficulty and in a short time. To one who had been on the fringe of the frantic and prolonged efforts of the previous appeal this was surprising, almost beyond belief. Nor did it prove any more credible when reported to the Executive Committee.

But then Ian Parry, who was soon to succeed Arthur Jones as Chairman of the Society, was travelling north with his wife Queenie and paused for tea in Lancaster. There they happened to meet two members of the Lancaster Footlights Club who had shared festival dates with the Tudor Players and thus knew the Parrys well. They told how their Club had taken over a defunct cinema in the town, purchased and renovated it, and opened it as their own amateur theatre. This they had achieved in the space of a few months with the aid of a fund-raising consultant named Thwaites. This also was reported back to the Society.

Despite misgivings on the part of most of the older members, Mr Thwaites was invited to visit Harborough and give his opinion. Meanwhile Alec, with characteristic short-fused enthusiasm, pressed ahead with designs for an enlarged theatre, cantilevered as suggested by Smiths, with a raised roof and extra backstage space, and he produced a scale-model to let people see what could be done.

One evening on his way home from London to Cockermouth Bill Thwaites stopped in Market Harborough, took a turn round the town and then met a few of the Society's officers in the Theatre. He asked some pertinent questions about membership, about support from the town and about programmes of activity and then said without hesitation, that £50,000 would not be enough but that one of his staff, lodged for a month in the town and given specified support from the members, could run a successful campaign to raise twice that amount. How could his be done ? Ah, that was not for disclosure until a contract had been agreed. But his calm confidence was persuasive.

So a special General Meeting was convened and the proposals explained. The response was chilly. There were those who had experience (or hearsay) of clubs that had hired a fund-raiser who had raised little more than his own fee. The Society's total reserves amounted to some £8,000. The costs of the campaign would eat up a large slice of this, Whilst the committed few pressed for the advantages of the rebuilding they failed to carry the day. The risk was too great.

A phone call to Thwaites to convey this decision was met with another surprise. He would put his man in for a fortnight and if at the end of that time it appeared that the target was not likely to be reached he would withdraw and make no charge other than the local expenses incurred. It was an offer that was difficult to refuse. So the little group that had been conducting the negotiations – Chairman, past Chairman, Treasurer, Artistic Director, Lettings Officer – took it on themselves to agree.

As so often in the democratic process, once bold leadership is seen it generates its own following. An appeal committee was formed with the past Chairman at its head and a series of meetings was called to carry out the initial preparation specified by Thwaites. These released a surprising reservoir of energy among the members, though it has to be said that some of the most responsible, especially some who had been deeply involved in the finances of the previous appeal, remained unconvinced.

Within a few days Freddie Markham, the Thwaites man, set up his office on the stage and started his training of the helpers. The fund was to be raised mainly by covenants, with the advantage of the tax refunds. At least one quarter of the target sum must be pledged by the members before an appeal could go out to townspeople and businesses. Invitations to buffet suppers were sent out to a wide range of people who had supported or had contact with the Theatre and those who came were shown round backstage so that they could appreciate the need for change. A list of likely subscribers was then prepared and shared out between some thirty members to be approached personally as they were trained to do by Markham.

Within four weeks some £80,000 had been pledged and a month

later the total was £99,971, just slightly short of the £100,000 target. It was undoubtedly the professionalism of Freddie Markham, his drive and tireless work, as well as his charm and sense of fun that enthused his band of co-workers and stilled the anxieties of the opposition. It was recognised that the Society had had good value for the £6,000 the campaign had cost. Most of the active work, however, was done by a small number of members who had appropriate personal or business contacts and were prepared to exploit them. A tablet showing the businesses contributing was prepared for display on the staircase when the building re-opened. Among them it was gratifying to see the generosity of the Harborough Mail which had been so long and so closely associated with the Society.

Old-style fund-raising events worked alongside: a big prize-draw, a lucrative bric-a-brac sale, exported shows like the Music Hall taken to the Rutland Sailing Club and to a children's party at Tungstone, a tour of villages with a Mummers Play (performed nearly everywhere in the pub because the weather was so bad) and the traditional coffee mornings carried on in the Old Grammar School.

Such events became even more necessary once building started. This was not until January 1981, a welcome delay because it put off the first payment. Since almost the whole fund was in the form of seven-year covenants there would be an immediate cash-flow problem when the bills came in. The target figure included interest on money borrowed but in the first year the cost of building would outstrip the likely scope of borrowing. In the end the matter was resolved by the generosity of a few members, notably the Chairman who personally guaranteed a bank loan of £10,000, and others who gave short-term interest-free loans to the Society. The financial control was overseen by O de Rousset Hall, recently replaced as President by Lieut-Colonel Derrick Hignett. It is entirely consistent with Tim de Rousset Hall's dedication to the Society, which he had served in so many capacities ever since 1946, that he should take on this task despite the deep disfavour with which he had initially regarded the whole scheme, and that he should now carry it through assiduously. Two others who merit special mention at this time are Freda Archer, the Treasurer, who handled all the complications of the covenants and tax refunds, and Ann Height, who as Lettings Officer had to manage the relationship with all those who normally used the Theatre for one purpose or another and whose patterns of activity were disrupted by the building work.

The Chairman determined that, as far as possible, the Society should remain "open". So, while excavations for the massive steelwork were going on below, the Theatre upstairs was brought back into use unexpectedly for an Old Time Music Hall that raised a commendable sum. Then, when the roof was taken off and the ground-floor trenches had been filled in, the Coffee Lounge came into use again. So plays could be given there, though on one night heavy rain poured in and the audience sat among buckets padded with tea-cloths to deaden the noise.

The programme for that season, 1980/81, reveals the ingenuity that had to be used to keep "open". First there was an Ayckbourn double-bill, *A Talk in the Park* and *Gosforth's Fete,* held in the garden of a member. Then David and Maggie Neal turned up with a show called *The Conjur'd Spirit,* compiled by David Neal. It was the story of Jonathan Swift and his love for those he called Stella and Vanessa. The roof was still on and so this was given on the stage upstairs. It was followed in November by *Murder in the Cathedral* in the Parish Church where, the pulpit and prayer-desks being on castors, a reasonable acting area can be created in front of the chancel arch. By mid-January the roof was still on and, as already told, the Music Hall could use the stage. Then when the roof was off, three productions took place downstairs: Pinter's *The Lover* which had to have an extra night to cope with the demand; the sodden evenings of Coward's *Still Life* and Priestley's *The Rose and Crown,* complete with buckets; and a triple bill that included Strindberg's *The Stronger* and Mankowitz's *Bespoke Overcoat.* All these were a sell-out. The appeal had been great publicity.

It was now May and the building was completely unusable. So the season ended with another Ayckbourn, *Round and Round the Garden* appropriately in the President's garden at East Langton Grange. This was a memorable show. June gave good weather and the facade of the house made a fine background fur the stage; but there was nowhere to hide a prompter and the cast had to do without. More than that, the garden looks out across the valley where the main line to London runs and every twenty minutes the cast had simply to freeze while a train went by. Surprisingly this upset no one. Cast and audience took it quite in their stride.

Building was held up by a hiccup in the supply of steelwork and by some bad weather and it became clear that the proposed handing over in August would not be achieved. Also a fairly late change in the plans allowed a tiered auditorium to be included. Some reconditioned tip-up seats from an old cinema were secured at the reasonable price of £20 per seat: ten rows of them with eleven or twelve to a row. Originally the fixing of the seats was to have been one of the members' DIY jobs but time was pressing and the contractors put them in. Because the cinema had had curved rows there was great difficulty in fitting the seats to the Theatres straight rows and the working party were much relieved to have been spared the task.

The opening of the new Theatre had therefore to be put back to November. The ground floor had not been changed much but the theatre upstairs was completely transformed. It was several feet wider, being built out over the toilets; the roof was higher; the tiered auditorium with proper theatre seats and the solid proscenium, which now had an opening of satisfying proportions, gave the impression of a real theatre. The stage was wider and deeper than before, with a solid cyclorama at the back and much more headroom for the lighting. New ten-foot flats had to be made in place of the old eight-footers, and over the backstage area was a large shelf or upper floor for storage. But there was still no appreciable wing-space and the wall at stage-left contained an awkward projection of brickwork that further restricted access on that side. Moreover although the roof had been lifted by several feet there was not quite enough height to fly scenery.

Throughout September and October 1981 working-parties laboured with the decoration and fitting out, first downstairs where the scars and splashes of the building-work had to be made good, and then upstairs where everything was new. Complete re-wiring was necessary, especially for the stage lighting which now required much heavier supplies of current, and there wasn't time for the lighting crew to do this. Contractors had to be brought in. New carpets were purchased and laid, and fittings for a wardrobe were installed in the space under the raised floor of the auditorium. All these were extra to the basic building cost but thanks to the way the covenanted payments came in and to prudent financial management they could be absorbed, for the initial loans and mortgage were paid off more quickly than had been calculated.

One disappointment remained, however. The way into the auditorium now involved an upper flight of stairs, making access for the disabled even more awkward than in the old building. To counter this, Queenie Parry had raised a separate sum for the specific purpose of putting in a lift; but when the plans had been agreed the Fire Officer vetoed them on the ground that escape in the event of an emergency would be impaired. So this matter of access remains an embarrassment.

Nevertheless all who have seen the rebuilt Theatre have been impressed with it. Newcomers are surprised to find so complete a theatre in such a building and the Society has every reason to be proud of it. This is especially so, since the design and structure were worked out, not by a firm of architects but by consultation between the Society's Artistic Director, Alec Riddett, and the builders, H J Smith and Son: a collaboration that worked splendidly, for Herbie Austin and his men contributed far more in the way of advice and planning than their contract called for. And those long-serving members who had laboured so valiantly with the old theatre, and with all the fund-raising that had gone on over the years, found themselves dazzled by their new home and agog with excitement at the opportunities it promised.

Merchant of Venice 1989

Mark Bodicoat as Lady Macbeth

Jeanne Moore in Ferndale … Macbeth

George Crossley in Old Time Music Hall

Virtue in Danger 1983

Gill Lucchesi in 84 Charing Cross Road 1990

Alan Atkins in Peter Pan 1991

Ruth Moore and Dave Wortley in Peter Pan 1991

ACT V ACTOR-MANAGERS (1981-1993)

The play selected for the opening of the new Theatre was Feydeau's classic farce *Hotel Paradiso,* which has a large cast, many scenes and a lot of typically farcical business between adjoining rooms. Here was something to display the expanded opportunities of the expanded stage and Ian Parry's racy production certainly did that. The stage crew, still struggling with the final phase of decorating and fitting out, had to build a complicated set with hinged walls that could be swung one way or the other to create different rooms and ingenious openings through which furniture could be quickly moved into the still limited space off-stage.

The first three performances, before booking was opened to the public, were given to invited audiences of covenanters to the appeal. Their delight at the outcome was echoed by the press review: "Now Harborough has a theatre where theatre-going is an undoubted pleasure – and the Drama Society has a worthy setting in which to parade its remarkable range of talents." No one entering the Theatre and looking down the wide rows of seats towards the proscenium could easily visualise the narrow tapering hall that was previously there. The pride of the stewards as they ushered the guests to their seats was evident and justified.

The same feeling of freedom granted by the new spaciousness characterised much of the season's offerings. *Cinderella,* devised and produced by O de Rousset Hall and Gwen Hudson, re-created the fun of their earlier pantomimes but with more spectacle and bigger troupes of dancers – 36 of them playing alternate nights half and half. Soon after, Gill Leftwich, who had played Prince Charming, brought her Opera Minima group for three nights of opera; then a studio triple bill of short plays, the tour of the Mummers' Play, a powerful production of *The Crucible,* Agatha Christie's *The Hollow* and John Osborne's *The Entertainer*; and the season ended with *Ten of the Best* by the Couronne Ballet School, and *The Snow Queen* by members of the County Youth Theatre selected, directed and publicised by Colin Window, a total of ten shows in a season that had not started until November. That is a record not equalled in any other season, but it is exactly what a theatre like this is for.

The next season, 1982/83, was even busier. The six full productions – an Ayckbourn, Priestley's *Dangerous Corner* (again), *Aladdin, Wild Goose Chase,* Tennessee Williams's *Glass Menagerie* and a rumbustious musical Version of Sir John Vanbrugh's *The Relapse* called *Virtue in Danger* – were supplemented by the Youth Theatre from Robert Smyth School with N F Simpson's *Was He Anyone?* by Northampton Repertory Company's *Rattle of a Simple Man* and the Leicester Flying Phoenix's *Taste of Honey.* The appeal for funds had promised that the rebuilt theatre would be a centre for the arts. The promise was now being fulfilled, for the Art Club and the Photographic Society contributed exhibitions during the run of plays and a proposal was made that films should be shown since the Ritz Cinema, the only survivor in town, had closed. Moreover, fortnightly Jazz Nights had been introduced, with live bands performing in the Lounge downstairs. These proved popular and brought in audiences not previously involved with the Theatre.

There followed the Golden Jubilee season, 1983/84. The eight plays ventured into an even wider range, beginning conventionally enough with Ayckbourn's *Living Together* but going on with the controversial *Killing of Sister George;* then Pamela Hansford Johnson's *Corinth House,* a drama of great charm and tenderness. Instead of a pantomime the Christmas show was a gallop over *50 Years of Golden Musicals,* produced by Pauline Moore; there was a Maugham, *The Constant Wife,* and a Coward, *Relative Values.* But the high spot of the season, advertised as The Jubilee Production, was a double bill of a novel kind, proposed and directed by Queenie Parry, namely *Hamlet* and Tom Stoppard's *Rosencrantz and Guildenstern Are Dead* performed end to end. The Stoppard play uses the same characters as Shakespeare but with a wholly different emphasis: in *Hamlet* the Prince's two friends, Rosencrantz and Guildenstern, have little to do but wait (and spy) on him. Stoppard makes this enforced idleness the centre of his play as the two characters talk to relieve their boredom and observe perfunctorily the great events of Shakespeare's tragedy – until they themselves are caught up in it. The casting was the same in the two plays; the characters are the same; but the weight of the parts is quite different. The Stoppard play ran first. Audiences might have found its ironies and innuendoes easier to grasp if *Hamlet* had been first; but altogether it was an impressive Jubilee presentation, rivalled in the Society's history only by Joan Norman's 1964 production of *Hamlet and The Dream* on alternate nights.

The season saw a number of new faces: John and Jan Bass, Jeanne and Robert Moore, Liz Deacon, Dai Perry, Alison Parkes, Beryl Spokes – and Alf Barber who also gave great service as Theatre Manager. Not only did he do up the kitchen but he badgered the District Council into grant-aiding the installation of a hearing loop for the benefit of patrons with hearing-aids.

Another innovation was a visit from the Hopscotch Theatre Group who gave three performances in one day for parties from local primary schools. Such missionary work among a future generation of theatre-goers is very important but theatre-in-education groups find it difficult to keep going for long and this particular experiment has never been repeated. However, the Jazz Nights continued successfully and the biggest ever social event was a Medieval Banquet when 120 members, appropriately garbed, were seated in the Lounge and fed by the Social Committee whose serving wenches were put under great pressure as they squeezed between the tables. Lettings to outside bodies and private parties were also increasing so that the consequent income became an important component of the annual accounts.

One consequence of the rebuilding of the Theatre was more assiduous attention from the Fire Officer – or the succession of Fire Officers, each appearing to have more stringent demands than the last. The ban on smoking throughout the Theatre – backstage and auditorium – took a long time to enforce and led to friction between the Fire Officer and the Theatre Manager and in turn between the Manager and producers. The last place to capitulate seems to have been the lighting box which has the feeling of a private cell insulated from the world beyond. The whole question of safety assumed greater prominence. An additional fire-exit had to be put in back- stage. The steel plates of the external fire-escape began to sag a little and collect pools of water when it rained. If these then froze the whole structure became treacherous; so drain-holes had to be drilled in the plates. Some of the sets on the new stage could be dressed with elegant and expansive curtains, often borrowed from someone's home. They all had to be sprayed with fire-proofing liquid. Fortunately not many plays call for a gun but when they do the regulations are tiresome. Moreover, the blanks that have to be used are not a ways reliable and that actor's nightmare has been not unknown when he fires at his enemy and his murderous intent is rewarded with a dull click. Once, to make quite sure, the stage manager fired a second revolver simultaneously behind the scene, but alas the resulting spray of gunpowder burnt a hole in the flat. Poison, or failing that a dagger, are to be preferred where possible.

There was a thought to extend the run to a full week starting on Monday night. This was rejected partly because the first nights (Tuesday) were not always full, but chiefly because Monday was the practice night for the parish church bellringers. They generously desisted for the Monday performances of the pantomimes but could not be expected to do the same for a whole season. So for the 1984/85 season the customary six plays ran for five nights only, apart from *Dick Whittington* which had fourteen. John Bass's fearsome King Rat in that show is still remembered: shuddering children were only with difficulty reassured by his wife Jan as the Fairy Queen.

One of the productions, a double bill of one-act plays, was given in the Lounge for the benefit of those who found the stairs up to the Theatre a deterrent. The plays ran for four nights at a special price of 50p. They were well supported and have become a regular feature of the annual programme. The final play that year was a revival of *Our Town* directed by Joan Norman (as she had in 1953) despite the disability that had caused her retirement from producing some years before. The season also included a visit from the Derby Playhouse with *The Late Late Christmas Carol,* from the Northampton Royal with *Affairs of State,* and from the Couronne Ballet School again with *Footloose and Fancy Free.*

The end of the season however was lit up by another surprise. The County Council, wishing to celebrate the 500th anniversary of the Battle of Bosworth Field which ended the Wars of the Roses, asked the Society for a production of Shakespeare's *Richard III* to be given at the battlefield in August 1985. This was undertaken by Queenie Parry and involved almost the entire active membership of the Society. The County's contractors put in tiers of seats and a stage floor but everything else, such as lighting and scenery, was provided by the Society. The backcloth, thirty feet long, designed and painted by Alec Riddett, was set up in three sections, the centre part of which now hangs on the stairs at the Theatre.

Like so many outdoor productions this one had to contend with wind, rain and cold, especially during rehearsals. (There had been a sort of dry run some years before, when one act of *Richard III* and a one-act play by David Campion had been given by the Society at Bosworth Field. That had been in June and it was perishing cold then.) In the event only one performance was seriously marred by rain, when the second half had to be transferred to the refreshment tent, and the whole venture was enormously successful, as the press notices reveal: "The hundreds who braved cold winds to watch the four open-air performances. . .were captivated by the high standard of acting and the company's pluck." For a while afterwards all those who had taken part in *Richard III* felt themselves, like Henry V's troops at Agincourt, a band of brothers who had braved the fire of battle and come through.

In other respects too success was in the air. The debts on the building had now been cleared and extensive renovation of the Lounge and bar had been completed, costing £4,000. With the cooperation of an arts club in Northampton, thus halving the hiring charges, a programme of films was prepared for the following season, a development that had been talked about for some time. Unfortunately the cult films chosen by the other group proved unattractive and after a disappointing response to the first two shows the idea was abandoned.

Now another problem arose. A consequence of the rebuilding was the diminished interest in the old Club Room which had been so significant in the life of the Society. Its upper floor had been fitted with racks and shelves to house the growing wardrobe: now there was a wardrobe under the auditorium, much more cramped but drier and much more convenient. The ground floor continued to be used for storing flats, furniture and props: now there was storage space on the upper floor behind the stage, not sufficient but handier. Moreover the old building was deteriorating. The stairs, always a bit springy, had to be propped up with spare lengths of 4 x 3; an upstairs window was rotting; and worst of all the roof developed a number of holes. The whole structure was so uncertain that it proved difficult to find a contractor who would venture on the roof. Eventually one did but the repairs were no more than temporary.

Nevertheless storage space was vital. A typical problem was

that of the Jazz Nights for which the visiting hands expected to perform on a stage, however minimal. Now in 1978 for his production of *View from the Bridge* Bryan Southwell had procured from the Haymarket Theatre some old rostra that had then been cut down to form a set of varying sizes. These have been a flexible resource ever since and they were used for the jazz players. The trouble was that they are bulky, heavy to carry and awkward to store and often there was nowhere for them but in the Club Room. Then it usually fell to Ken Cooper, instigator and organiser of the Jazz Nights, to do the carrying which, especially late at night after a jazz performance, was a hardly acceptable labour. No wonder that he tried to persuade the Society to put up a permanent platform in the Lounge, but that would have made more problems than it solved.

Hence when Webbs' outfitters by whose goodwill the Club Room had been occupied, closed down in 1986 and the property was to be sold, the question of purchase was raised. Those who were concerned, especially the stage crew who needed the storage, argued for purchase but the likely cost of restoration – and be it said the indifference with which the Club Room was viewed by a majority of members by this time – scuppered the idea. Enquiries were made locally to find an alternative store but without success (one empty property was offered at a price of £140,000) until an approach to St Luke's Hospital up the Leicester Road gained access to the old casual ward, a l930s building now unoccupied and partly derelict.

Here, in return for a nominal donation, was ample space and the offer was taken up gladly, although the building was a long way from the Theatre, the roof leaked, there was no lighting, and holed windows meant that the accommodation was shared with tribes of starlings who added their decorations to everything stored there. However, a whole Sunday was spent with a borrowed van transferring the Society's treasures to this new home.

Hardly was this done than the Youth Training Scheme, also in search of premises, took over the whole building, set their trainees on a complete restoration, and turned the Drama Society out. A small corner of a garage on the site was provided as an alternative but a great deal of the Society's stock had simply to go to the tip. This limited space at St Luke's silts up with props and units of scenery every season and has to be ruthlessly culled at least once a year; it is too far away to be as convenient even as the old Club Room, but it has to suffice. Because of its central site the Theatre cannot expect to find a space nearby at a price it could afford.

Not that the Society was now poor. Having cleared the mortgage earlier than expected, as interest rates had fallen, there was a surplus by the time the covenants were completed. This served to replace the sum originally drawn from the Theatre Account to pay for the professional appeal, for it was clear that from time to time heavy outlay would have to be faced for maintenance. The day-to-day running was now over £6,000 per year before any activities began. The plays roughly broke even; bar profits, coffee mornings and lettings provided a cushion; so prudence in expenditure was felt to be paramount, especially as the total turnover was coming close to the point at which VAT would be incurred. Between 1986 and February 1988 when registration for VAT had to be done, an anxious watch was kept on finances. The Theatre was now not just a place for acting, nor just an arts centre: it was very much a business calling for effective management.

Fortunately this period of the Society's growth was guided by a succession of unusually competent officers: Freda Archer as treasurer and then as chairman, John Bass who succeeded her as treasurer, and Ann Height who followed as chairman.

Fortunately too the Society's creative life was being well managed. For instance, when Alec Riddett's new job caused him to give up as Artistic Director, Trevor Brown immediately stepped in. When his new job did the same he was followed by Cliff Hudson, and as scene-painter by Carole White, daughter of Bertie Norman who had set such a standard of scenic design all those years ago. More recently Pat Hipple has come in as designer, sharing the painting with Carole, and George Crossley has taken over as coordinator of the construction crew.

But in 1985 sudden casting problems had caused the cancellation of *Death of a Salesman* at a quite late stage and although the slot in the programme was hastily filled with a couple of one-act plays this unaccustomed disaster led to a serious review of production arrangements. One important decision was that each production should have a member of the Production Committee to look in on its progress and offer help if difficulties should arise. In this and other ways the involvement of the Committee was sharpened and the results can be seen in the seasons that followed.

The range of plays chosen was as broad and as adventurous as ever, as can be seen from a selection from the next few seasons' programmes, each having the usual six or seven productions. That for 1985/86 included *Abigail's Party, Outside Edge* and *Hobson's Choice;* the next year *Pack of Lies, On Golden Pond* and *Lord Arthur Savile's Crime.* The list then ranges from contemporary plays like *Dangerous Obsession* or *The Exorcism* to *The Farmer's Wife,* or Becket's *Happy Days,* or D H Lawrence's *Widowing of Mrs Holroyd;* from *Under Milk Wood* to *Oh What a Lovely War* and a reversion to old times with *Mother Goose,* a pantomime devised and produced by O de Rousset Hall; from a *Merchant of Venice* set in Docklands or Pinter's The *Betrayal* to perhaps the most hilarious show (and the longest title) ever staged by the Society, *The Farndale Avenue Housing Estate Townswomen's Guild Dramatic Society's Production of Macbeth.*

A growing demand for tickets brought up again the question of extending the run of the plays. For most of its life the Society has been indebted to Greens, the High Street stationers, who have generously acted as honorary booking agents. Tickets have always gone on sale there three weeks before opening night but now a number of productions sold out within a week and for the pantomimes a proportion of matinee tickets had to be held back for individual patrons because of the rush of block bookings from children's organisations, all of which regrettably caused embarrassment to Greens. Eventually it was decided to brave the bellringers and open some productions on a Monday. It was found that the bells were hardly noticed.

Not only audiences were being attracted. Once more new talent was emerging: Tony Birchall, Chris Ward, John Mayor, Robert Parkes, Gill Lucchesi, Frank Avery, Sean Fountain, Mark Bodicoat, Les Dodd, Dave Wortley, Gill Totten, Roger Fry, George Crossley, Alan Atkins, and in the lighting box Simon Malin and Richard Simpkin all appeared for the first time during these seasons. But in the long run the most important step in recruiting new talent may prove to be the Junior Stage Workshop started by Charlotte Bodicoat and Di Rickard.

There was another production that almost faced cancellation – and also met the problem of disappointed customers through an early sell-out. That was *Rebecca* in 1985. John Bass in the lead, struggling against the illness that later was to prove fatal, carried on bravely right up to the dress rehearsal but then could go on no longer. John Burgess, not seen on the Harborough stage for some years, came in at a few hours' notice to take the part – with a book – and the play went on. But it was a sad time for the Society. In the previous year Richard Hill, a much respected member who for years had operated the sound equipment, had died suddenly. Shortly afterwards Wendy Dodd, newly elected as secretary, and John Bass the treasurer, died in the prime of life. A further unexpected loss was Tony Saggers whose virtuosity at the piano had imparted great vitality to pantomimes and musical shows. A *Cinderella* that he had written was included in the 1989/90 season, a fitting memorial for it was full of life and fun, as Tony himself had been.

Throughout this period the Theatre was heavily used. Among visiting companies were the Derby Playhouse with *Lady Chatterley's Lover* and London Connection with two one-woman plays entitled *A Talent to Influence.* The Northampton Royal Theatre brought *The Old Curiosity Shop* and Valentine Pelka, a member of the Royal Shakespeare Company, gave a dramatic performance of Tennyson's *Maud.* At the 1986 AGM it was reported that during the year a total of thirty-six organisations had used the Theatre, mainly the Lounge. An attempt was made to hold the Jazz Nights weekly but there were problems with other users and they became fortnightly again. A play-reading group was formed, but met with a rather disappointing response. A Poetry Group, however, formed in 1987 is flourishing still.

Charitable projects also continued. The annual carol-singing round the town has raised considerable sums for CARE Village, as has the Society's stall at the CARE Summer fete. Ever since 1980, by Cliff Hudson's initiative, the Society has provided two teams for the weekly Talking Newspaper for the Blind. For at least one play a year a gala night, with supper, has been given for a local charity. A special performance of *Whose Life is it Anyway?* raised £300 for the Market Harborough Hospital Appeal, and a recital organised by the Poetry Group raised almost £200 for the Jubilee Sailing Trust to enable a disabled member to join a voyage in the "Winston Churchill" sailing ship. For several years the Rotary Club sponsored a special performance of one of the plays as part of their charitable work. In these and other ways the relationship between the Theatre and the town, which had been so crucial to the two appeals, was being honourably sustained.

Meanwhile some further improvements were undertaken. The stonework of the facade was cleaned, a complete face-lift was given to the Coffee Lounge, and a new electronic lighting control board was installed. This last, together with improved sound equipment and the upgrading of the wiring to new standards set by the local authority, cost over £7,000 which shows how wise it was to husband the financial reserves. Hopes still linger that some adjoining space might become available to relieve the pressure backstage and in the dressing room – of which there is only one, a unisex that becomes impossibly crowded when there is a large cast – and perhaps to improve the toilet facilities. The longing for improvement will never be satisfied but it is prudent to hold reserves for any prospect that may arise.

As has been said, the Drama Society has become a business, a business with a large annual turnover and considerable capital assets. The major asset is the Theatre itself, acquired through the dedicated work of the members and the generosity of the people of Market Harborough. That is the Society's heritage. Creating it and managing it for the benefit of the town has been a long learning process for the whole membership, especially with the enhanced opportunities of the rebuilt Theatre. The record shows how well those opportunities have been taken.

EPILOGUE

Looking back over the records of sixty years one is struck by several things. First, how steadily forward has been the progress. The Drama Society would not be human without its ups and downs; but the downs seem always to have stimulated a new up so that development, whether structural or artistic, quickly resumed.

Secondly, how strong has been the collective bond between members, Whenever a special effort was called for a good response was found. That is not unusual. But an operation like the Theatre depends on very many people shouldering regular and often humdrum jobs, and going on doing so. A rough calculation of the demands of a pantomime like the 1993 *Aladdin,* which ran for two weeks with a cast of 21, shows that there had to be a further 23 support staff – backstage, lighting, music, wardrobe, set builders – and altogether 70 front-of-house (house manager, stewards, programme-sellers, coffee-makers, bar staff). In all, they gave over 3,000 man-hours, 1,300 in rehearsals and 1751 in the run itself. Even a two-hander like *Happy Days* tots up some 400 man-hours. This has been going on up to six, seven, eight times a year for most of the sixty years. Add all the work of maintenance, decorating, improvements, publicity, coffee mornings, socials, and so on, and the sum of individual commitment is huge.

Thirdly, the Society has maintained its strength despite the inevitable loss of members from many causes. The programmes list a total of almost 700 acting members over the whole period. Some of these appear once only, inviting speculation about the reasons. But the pool of talent is always topped up by new people. The Society remains a force greater than the sum of its individuals.

Finally, the Society has never lost sight of its wider responsibility but has always sought to enrich the cultural and artistic life of the town. Amateur drama faces the constant temptation towards self-indulgent exhibitionism, seeing the next production as the be-all and end-all of its concern. The Harborough Society has been saved from that trap by the chance opportunities of leasing, buying and then building its own theatre. It has had to recognise its dependence on its fellow townspeople, offering them not a stage to display its own feathers but a multi-purpose arts centre which engages with their concerns, which has room for other arts and a welcome for other companies. At the same time, in its own work, it has held fast to the high standards of its origins, leading rather than following the tastes of the day. If ever the Society loses that breadth of purpose it will forfeit its claim to the backing of its public.

The record of these sixty years is a story of remarkable achievement attained, one might say, by Roger Ascham's formula of "good behaviour and audacitie". May that continue to be the watchword as the Market Harborough Drama Society marches on towards its centenary.

STAGE BY STAGE – 1993 -2008

The diamond jubilee was a momentous landmark for the drama society. What began as a small drama class trying its hand at George Bernard Shaw in 1933, had evolved into a thriving community theatre group, and it was undoubtedly a time for celebration.

Sixty years of performing in Market Harborough, was commemorated with a celebratory party at The Nutmeg Tree pub (now The Peacock) and an exhibition in the theatre lounge.

Attending an opening event for the exhibition was former Market Harborough Drama Society player David Neal, who, after first appearing on stage in the town in 1969, turned professional and went on to appear in films such as *Superman, Flash Gordon* and television shows *Doctor Who, Inspector Morse* and *Poirot*. Roy McCready, another member who turned professional, also attended.

The book *Stage By Stage*, compiled by theatre stalwart Arthur Jones, and charting the history of the society from its early days was published to mark the diamond jubilee and a season of repeat performances was planned.

The local newspaper revealed how the society would be "reviving memories of the good old days", but the idea of repeating past plays was not favoured by all. The society, after all, had always prided itself on innovation and a desire to take on new challenges. But a season of reprisals was by no means a soft option, with testing works planned from the pens of Shaw, Wilde and Shakespeare.

The new season started where it had all begun – with a much-anticipated performance of George Bernard Shaw's *Candida*.

Shaw's tale of Christianity, socialism and feminism was of course the society's first ever play in 1933, back when Harold Jones was breathing life into a languishing little theatrical group borne out of Leicester's Little Theatre which would go on to become Market Harborough Drama Society.

Bryan Southwell's 1993 production starred Nadine and James Scott, Dave Wortley and Philip Smart and seemed to strike a chord with a modern audience with reviews noting how the play "explored issues which still have relevance today."

At the time, performances were playing to audiences reaching 85-90% capacity on average. This compared with London theatre audiences of 69% and the rest of the UK at 58%.

Theatre was thriving in Market Harborough and box-office takings from each play were averaging about £2,000.

Despite a certain amount of financial security, it was important the society didn't rest on its laurels, but continued to stretch itself creatively.

Embodying this ethic, Bunty Jones made her debut in the costume department, charged with the unenviable task of creating the requisite costumes of ancient Byzantine times for Shakespeare's *A Winter's Tale*.

Thanks to a sale at Homebirds of West Langton and another at Welland Separates in St Mary's Road, Harborough, as well as forays to a number of fabric warehouses, Bunty gathered more than 150 yards of appropriate materials from which she fashioned some 45 costumes for the cast of 27.

The ensemble piece – brought to the stage with the combined efforts of Bunty and producers Arthur Jones and Jan Bass – was rightly hailed by reviewers as "a triumph" and "an example of the society at its best."

The festive season brought us *Beauty and the Beast* with David Wortley taking on the role of the lesser attractive titular protagonist. Complete with a contemporary twist and "naughty jokes", it proved a huge hit with children and adults alike.

The society then went back to school with John Dighton's farce *The Happiest Days of Your Life* – a forerunner to the *St Trinian's* films. One amusing moment during the play happened when a sound effect of a car pulling up was late. When the actor said "I think they have arrived now…" the lighting box remembered to put the sound effect on and the other actor ad-libbed "you've got far better hearing than I have!"

Alan Window directed Agatha Christie's *Murder At The Vicarage* with Betty Whitelaw receiving rave reviews as Miss Marple, a performance said to have rivalled that of television's Marple Joan Hickson!

Liz Deacon got to utter the famous line "A handbag?!" for a

second time as she once again took on the role as Lady Bracknell in Wilde's *The Importance of Being Earnest*.

Under Jeanne Moore's direction, Liz showed she had nothing to declare but her genius as she gave a commanding performance. In fact, one reviewer quipped her Lady Bracknell gave the audience a glimpse of what it must have been like to be a "lacklustre minister in Margaret Thatcher's cabinet"!

In September 1994, Harborough Theatre completed a much-needed renovation, at a cost of £70,000. It was mostly funded by the society's repairs and renewals reserves built up over the past decade.

The makeover included interior design and redecoration of the auditorium, foyer, bar-lounge and kitchen, re-upholstered seating, complete carpeting, and soundproofing of the lighting and sound control room.

The toilets were also upgraded for play-goers, the lounge floor was relaid and the dressing room enlarged.

The project was helped by donations. Grants were also awarded by Harborough District Council (which also contributed with an interest-free loan), the Sports and Arts Foundation, Garfield Weston Trust, Hanson Trust, Col D Hignett, Hickinbotham Trust, and Councillor J Shaw.

Stephen Harrison, who was stage-managing the first play of the new season, enthused publicly that he felt the work had "given the theatre a tremendous lift."

And Michael Baatz added: "I think most of the society's members think that it is a very satisfactory and pleasant refurbishment for both the actors and the audience."

The society understandably used the facelift as a ploy to get more punters through the door and urged people to come and visit the theatre and judge the renovation work for themselves. It was also hoped the work would encourage more visiting production companies to come and perform here.

This revamp, however, was relatively small fry compared to what would follow over the coming years.

When the Olivier award winning play *My Mother Said I Never Should* was staged, with Nadine Scott, Gill Lucchesi, Sarah Moore and Alison Dodd, it proved to be a "brave and superbly executed opener to Harborough Drama Society's season."

Brave, no doubt, because it would include a controversial use of the 'f-word'. It wasn't the first time the word had been used on the Harborough stage. The rather dubious first was notched up in 1987 when it was said in *Whose Life Is It Anyway?*

However, in *My Mother Said I Never Should* it had to be said by a character played by a young Alison Dodd (then 15 years old). The use of the expletive had concerned the drama committee at the time which suggested cutting it. But director Jan Wilson fought to keep it in as she felt it was integral to the script.

It wasn't the last time the f-word would cause some concern.

Michael Frayn's *Noises Off*, directed by Jan Wilson, opens with an unforgettable use of the word, blurted out by a character 'planted' in the audience who has to yell "Get off the ******* stage!".

Nick Lewis, who had to utter the phrase, had understandably been a little reluctant to say the line, but he and director Jan Wilson eventually decided Frayn's shock-tactic should remain.

Since then, the use of strong language on the Harborough Theatre stage (notably in *Death And The Maiden*, which amusingly no-one wanted to prompt on because of the bad language!) has cropped up on various occasions as and when the script demands, but audiences have always seemed receptive to challenging, adult material.

On a more family-friendly note, pantomime season brought us *Dick Whittington* with Ruth Moore (who has appeared in over 40 plays for the society and also at Leicester's Little Theatre) as Dick.

Alison Dodd, Marilyn Holderness, Alan Window, Sue I'anson (in her debut) and Jeanne Moore (as Queen Rat) provided fun support.

The Lion In Winter, featured costumes from the RSC (acquired by director Gill Lucchesi) and in June 1995, a revival was in order when the society staged *The Boyfriend*, a frothy musical set in the fun-loving 1920s in the south of France. The show had proved so popular when it was last staged in 1977, that the brave step was taken to extend the run this time around.

Just as she did for Wilde's *Earnest* the previous year, Liz Deacon reprised a role she had played in the original staging of *The Boyfriend*. It was produced by the ever-busy Jeanne Moore and featured newcomer Wendy Lomas who would go on to appear on stage many times at the theatre and later direct.

To advertise the show, a replica photo was staged in full 20s regalia, almost identical to that which had appeared in 1977 on the front cover of the Northampton and County Independent magazine. A vintage car was even drafted in to help capture the authentic feel of the period.

The advertising campaign worked and *The Boyfriend* was a sell-out!

In autumn 1995, the Harborough Mail ran a feature about the theatre to coincide with the new season.

The article amusingly compared the theatre to Doctor Who's preferred method of transport the Tardis, due to it being a lot bigger on the inside than it looks from the outside. One suspects, even to this day, that those who have never ventured inside Harborough Theatre may still be shocked at the size of the facilities which lie behind the modestly-sized façade.

The article revealed that at this point in time, the drama society had about 200 members, of which about 50 had acted on stage. But it made no disguise of the fact that the society was actively seeking new members, particularly younger people (the perennial problem).

To achieve this it firstly needed to get young people to come and watch plays. This problem was illustrated when the society took a peek into *The Diary Of Anne Frank*, with Chloe Heatlie playing the title role and Alan Window and Gordon Henderson directing. (It was staged to mark 50 years since the end of World War II).

The results of a questionnaire carried out during the run showed that only 7% of the audience were under 18. This was despite the casting of three teenagers in the play and the fact it was being studied in local schools.

Paradoxically, the largest theatre-going group nationally is the under 21s, mainly due to their attendance at Christmas shows and set-text productions.

We therefore know there's a young audience out there, the question is, how to reach them?

The questionnaire also revealed that 70% of the *Anne Frank* week's audience were female.

Hence why the society was also seeking men at this time.

There had been a drop-off in the number of male actors joining the drama society and because most plays were written by men, with predominantly male leads, the need for more men to join was imperative.

Comments made by the then Publicity Officer Nick Lewis stressed that the drama society was open to all ages. There was a desire to shake off the perception that it was a "small and elitist group". As Nick insisted: "This is not a nest of luvvies!"

The theatre had arguably become the victim of a changing society. Pressures on young people's time were growing. The trend for young people to travel further to work, often commuting long distances, takes sizeable chunks of time out of one's day.

Young women were also returning to work much sooner after having children than in previous years. That trend continues to this day. In the past, young mums tended to take longer to return to work after giving birth, thus giving them more free-time to spend at the theatre. The theatre provided an ideal opportunity for non-working mums to enjoy some greatly-valued adult company.

Modern lifestyles have unfortunately made it difficult to juggle work, parenthood and leisure time. Many, however, do manage it, dedicating much of their time to the theatre, and for that the society is incredibly grateful.

To encourage greater involvement, the theatre was regularly opening its doors to wider sections of the community, including a poetry group, a play reading group and a Playworks group which experimented with directing, acting and the study of drama. There was a definite push, at this time, to increasing the number of groups and visiting productions. After all, we had a recently refurbished theatre to show-off and there was a strong urge that others should get to share in what it had to offer.

'Innnovations' – which consisted of members aged 18 to 30 and concentrated on musicals – and the Harborough Youth Theatre, which catered for youngsters aged 11 to 20, were two groups recently set up to encourage younger participation in theatre activities.

Meanwhile, the drama society looked to entice a younger audience through the doors when it took on *Toad Of Toad Hall* for the third time.

Kenneth Grahame's children's favourite had first been performed by the society in 1951. In fact, some of the players involved in that original production were still members when the show was reprised, namely Kate Plowman, Joan Norman, Joan's daughter Carole White and Betty Whitelaw. Carole had also been in the 1980 version and completed a hat-trick this time by playing the washerwoman. Susan Cooper was at the helm this time around, having previously been assistant director. Margaret Chapman played the bargewoman (a promotion from her previous role as one half of Fenella the horse!) and John Farnsworth appeared as Mole having played Toad in 1980.

The drama-making machine was in full motion, as ever, and as plays were being rehearsed, auditions were already being held for the next productions.

Society president, at the time, Freda Archer equated the experience to "a production line," saying, "In order to present the seven shows being staged this season, we have to plan ahead, completing the casting, choosing the helpers and advisors and starting rehearsals – all overlapping."

The "production line" continued with Neil Simon's comedy *Last of the Red Hot Lovers* which saw the society once again "coming up trumps" (according to one reviewer) with Dave Wortley splendidly portraying the lusty Barney, a character who, after 23 years of marriage, attempts to join the sexual revolution before it's too late.

Shortly after was a studio production of Jean Anouilh's *Antigone* – a modern interpretation of an ancient Greek tragedy.

Concerns had been raised that a weighty, period play such as *Antigone* would prove a "hard-sell" after the frothy delights of Neil Simon, but the audience did come and the play was a resounding success. "Riveting" enthused one reviewer, noting Tom Henderson's show stealing performance as King Creon.

Antigone was an example of the society's so-called 'studio productions' which run for fewer nights – downstairs in the theatre lounge – while offering the audience the chance to see rarely-performed or unusual plays which can be scheduled alongside more mainstream comedies and dramas.

Alan Window, production officer at the time, commented in the Mail that a studio production would involve "just as much work for the performers and supporting staff, but they allow us to provide a greater variety for our patrons."

Long-time society member and set designer Alec Riddett made a long-overdue return to the stage, albeit in a cameo role, in the darkly comic satire *The Physicists*. It also marked the debut of Allison Collier. They were joined by Frank Avery, Tim Bevin, Richard Bosworth, Jane Southwell, Jeremy Thompson and Gill Totten.

As the Euro '96 championships kicked off, those fleeing the apparent ubiquity of international football sought solace at the theatre and the society scored another winner with the delightful elementary school-set comedy (and indeed a play of two halves) *Daisy Pulls It Off*.

Tickets went like hot cakes and virtually sold out within a week of the box office opening.

This was great news for the Operatic Society who had teamed up with the Drama Society to organise the opening night as a fundraiser for Project 2001. This was raising money for the creation of the Octagon Theatre as one of the functions of a substantially re-built Octagonal Hall at Welland Park College.

It was a much-enjoyed show and – just like Daisy in the title (played by a debuting Claire Oakley) – the two societies' combined forces had indeed, pulled it off!

This was a fine example of cooperation and common interest between local arts groups, which the society had been striving for. The audience benefited too, both from a rattling good show and the knowledge that their ticket money was going to a worthy cause.

By this time, the Harborough Theatre Gala Night – whereby the society 'donates' a performance and use of the theatre to a local charity – had become an established fixture. Many local organisations had benefited from the gala nights over the years, a source of much pride amongst members, and rightly so.

With the arrival of Jack Booth in 1996, plans for the future of the theatre would become ever more ambitious. Jack had worked in shop interior design and construction most of his life – mainly for the Burton clothing group – and his technical expertise and natural interest in set design would help shape the future of the theatre, quite literally.

Jack, along with Nick Lewis and Dennis Davison, the new Theatre Manager, explored ways to expand and develop the theatre and over the coming years, they worked on feasibility studies to establish what the venue could achieve. Dennis had been in management with Mecca Ballrooms and brought this expertise to bear on the running of the theatre, which in turn prompted an elder statesman to describe him as "the best theatre manager we have had."

One of the big aims was for the society to acquire the shop next door to the theatre. This would effectively double the size of the theatre lounge, as well as providing potential for exhibition facilities, a meeting room and workshop.

It would be a laborious, and at times, frustrating process, but not one without results. It would all boil down to the bottom line – money – not to mention planning permission, so long-term strategies for bringing the expansion plans to fruition were set in motion.

Meanwhile, the shows must go on, and ever-looking to 'raise the bar', it was decided the 1996/1997 season would ambitiously include eight productions, two more than usual.

It promised a Dream start (with Shakespeare) right through to a Crisp finish (with N J Crisp's poignant *Fighting Chance*), with some Miller, Godber and Bennett thrown in for good measure.

The society began with Shakespeare's *A Midsummer Night's Dream* – but with a twist. Instead of the traditional production one might expect with the Bard, director Jan Wilson (who had drawn on influences from her time working with the Royal Shakespeare Company) chose to set it in the 1940s.

One clearly impressed member of the audience even sent a letter in to the Harborough Mail to profess how much she enjoyed this "brilliant performance" by such "talented artists" as Alex Reffel (who stepped in to play Helena after illness forced Elaine Kellman to pull out) Alan Atkins, Les Dodd, Chris Smith, Emily Freer and, of course, Mark Bodicoat's "swaggering" Bottom!

The theatre was ringing in the changes at this time when a new telephone system was launched to inform people about forthcoming performances or for people to get involved. The phone line ran a two minute message to publicise the next show and give information of last-minute ticket availability.

One problem at this time was, although home-produced plays were selling well, audiences for visiting productions were small. While drama society shows boasted well over 80 per cent attendance with frequent sell-outs, the last four visiting productions had only mustered between 25 and 50 patrons in a 118-seat auditorium. This was hugely disappointing for a society of over 220 members.

Hoping to buck the trend was award-winning playwright Lynn Robertson-Hay, who brought her visually-arresting one-woman show *Redeeming Features* to the theatre (it would return too in 2008 in support of Prostaid). Lynn was returning to her Harborough roots and was better known in the town as Lynn Parry, daughter of society stalwarts Ian and Queenie Parry.

Queenie Parry said: "The beauty of visiting productions is that, not only do they provide a financial boost for the theatre, they also provide added variety."

She said many professionals have performed at the theatre as part of visiting productions and society members can, and have, learned a great deal from seeing other groups perform. Even watching bad shows can be educational, she said.

To emphasise the theatre's role as a 'community theatre', efforts were made by the society's executive committee to increase interest and seek more talent locally who would be given guidance in bringing performances to the theatre. Offers from all angles were accepted and ideas put forward included attracting novice stand-up comedians, musicians for MTV-style "unplugged" events and for village drama groups to branch out by staging a show at Harborough Theatre.

Not all these ideas were realised, but some did come together, and the theatre would soon diversify to host comedy nights (with many top acts appearing) and, some years later, film screenings.

It seemed every inch of the theatre was being utilised where possible. John Godber's *Teechers* (yes, misspelled deliberately!) was produced in the studio bar, with three players Jan Wilson, Graham Day and Peter Edwins taking on no less than 19 roles in a single play. It was an ambitious project, but many felt that it could have warranted a performance on the main theatre stage, where it could have reached a wider audience.

Successfully concluding its ambitious eight show season, the society rewarded patrons by cutting the cost of annual season tickets, giving them the chance to catch the forthcoming eight shows of the 1997/98 season for the price of six.

High points of the season included Wendy Lomas's memorable turn going from hairdresser from hell to scholar in the two-hander *Educating Rita*. The rehearsal threw up a priceless spoonerism, said by Malcolm Hipple, who was playing opposite Wendy – instead of saying "Wordsworth tomb", he said "turdsworth womb". As the character was supposed to be drunk at the time, it was left in the play!

Then there was the unusually-titled comedy *The Woman Who Cooked Her Husband*, a play that proved that the way to a man's heart really was through his stomach. The title wasn't the only unusual thing about the play, as all the props were mimed.

(Jan Wilson had chosen to stage the self-confessed "peculiar" play, not only because it was unusual and challenging, but because she had known its author Debbie Issett at university).

Nick Lewis's production of Dickens' *A Christmas Carol* proved a festive delight and a younger generation of actors got to tread the boards when Market Harborough Drama Society's Youth Section – involving 11-18 year olds – staged the provocative and topical *Zigger Zagger*.

This told of the lives of football-crazed youngsters looking for work and fun, against a backdrop of violence on the terraces. A challenging play for any young actor, no doubt, in that it requires the audience to empathise with football hooligans. But Jan Wilson and Susan Cooper at the helm, and their young cast, achieved the desired effect.

The youth section had previously been overseen by Di Rickard and Jeanne Moore, but it was rejuvenated in the late 90s by Jan and Susan to encourage much needed younger actors to the theatre.

During its time, it would nurture the raw talents of Lee Brace, Dan Pelo and Simon Howard amongst others.

The group ran for a few years, putting on several workshops, but when job-relocation meant Susan had to move to New York, the running of the youth section proved increasingly demanding and time-consuming. Although *Zigger Zagger* was to be the youth section's only major production, it was a good example of how youngsters' enthusiasm for drama can be developed.

To encourage further local creativity, Harborough District Council linked up with the theatre to launch a project called Stageworks, which involved 30 people who took part in creative writing workshops at the theatre to produce over 20 original one-act plays.

Sadly, around this time, the society lost a number of key members with the deaths of long-time actress and director since the 1930s Joan Norman, lighting and sound wizard Norman Ward and regular actors Cliff Hudson and Bob Whitelaw. In the years to come, the society would also lose wonderful comic actress and singer Sheila Dean, talented actress Gill Totten, remembered for her huge sense of fun, and actor Chris Smith, who had appeared in plays *Midsummer Night's Dream* and *Double Cut*, but who died tragically from a bee sting.

On a happier note, ongoing plans to revamp the theatre took a huge leap forward when the society received news that the town's oldest charity, the Market Harborough and Bowdens Charity had agreed to plough £750,000 into four major projects in the town. One of these was the theatre extension.

Commenting at the time, the society said: "The extension would provide a facility for the whole community and we are delighted with the news of the grant."

The aim was still to raise enough money to buy the shop next door.

An initial feasibility study for this had been carried out by Len Bale and Jack Booth and a phased development programme for the building work was drawn up.

More good news followed when Harborough District Council's environment committee agreed in principle that the public toilets in Factory Lane, which had been closed due to frequent vandalism, could be incorporated into the theatre extension if the society was prepared to purchase them.

It was an exciting time as the theatre rolled on positively into the 1998/99 season which began in ship-shape fashion when a rousing production of the farce *Sailor Beware* opened to a full house. Works by Agatha Christie, Alan Bennett and JB Priestley would be tackled over the year ahead.

When the theatre called for adults and children to audition for the parts of "beavers, fawns, wolves, leopards, uglies, ghouls, dwarfs and even Father Christmas", it could only mean one thing – an imminent production of the ever-popular *The Lion, The Witch And The Wardrobe*. This delightful foray into the land of Narnia was particularly timely as it celebrated the centenary of C S Lewis's birth.

It would prove one of the theatre's most technically-challenging shows, with numerous scene changes, elaborate costumes and special effects, but set designer Jack Booth, director Margaret Humphrys and the stage management team were undaunted and rose to the occasion.

Scene painter Carole White, who was continuing the good work done behind the scenes by her father, painted the magnificent backdrop, drawn by Jack Booth. Carole's artistic fingerprints continue to appear on many a theatre set to this day.

Jeanne Moore stepped in at the eleventh hour to play the demanding role of the White Witch, after a family illness forced Linda De Gallier to pull out. Two prompts at each end of the stage and some carefully hidden scripts, just in case, were utilised during the production to help Jeanne if she forgot her lines. Of course, great performer that she is, she didn't need them.

Special rehearsals had to be called to ensure things went ahead. Margaret Humphrys said at the time: "I can't speak highly enough of the actors, from the oldest to the youngest, who dropped their Christmas arrangements to come in."

The end result was that the show was a sell-out.

On August 1st, 1999, a garden party was held at Arthur and Bunty Jones' house to celebrate the 90th birthday of Kate Plowman. Kate was of course a founder member of the Drama Society in 1933, and was still actively supporting it. Then chairman, Jan Bass, presented Kate with a bouquet of flowers on the day from the society. Kate would continue to support the society up until her death in 2003.

Like the previous season, the new one began with a farce – on this occasion *Fish Out Of Water*, which was, in the words of director Jan Wilson, a "jolly good romp with plenty of laughter!" Publicity for the show featured some pretty racy shots of a semi-clad Alison Dodd, who had just returned from three years at university to take on the role of a sexy Italian maid.

During the season, *The Railway Children* steamed along to the theatre, Godber's families were happy and JB Priestley's inspector called once again.

Anne Hepworth, who directed the latter, recalls how Tom

Henderson, who was starring as the play's patriarch, had terrible trouble learning his many lines and decided that, after around 100 stage appearances over the years, it would definitely be his last performance for the society and that he would "go out on a high!"

By far the most ambitious project of the season was dreamed up by Margaret Humphrys and George Kitson. Margaret had been a long-term member of the society, but George had only recently moved up from London where he ran the Central School of Speech and Drama, which had trained the likes of Judi Dench and Laurence Olivier. He had been invited to join the drama society in Harborough by his dentist – one Gordon Henderson!

Shakespeare and the Green Dragon, which featured scenes from a number of the Bard's plays, was written and directed by Margaret and George. The set recreated the inside of the Green Dragon inn in the year 1620, and was designed and constructed by Alec Riddett, Jack Booth and team.

The play was a millennium celebration of Shakespeare on the theme of love, and was based on local research – the Green Dragon in Church Square, of course, used to be where the theatre stands today. It was dubbed in the press "Shakespeare On Love!" and required the efforts of more than 20 people behind the scenes, resulting in a marvellous example of an original production borne out of the unique talents and creativity of local people.

On the eve of the new millennium, a memorable party had been held for members in the theatre lounge. Society member Martin Thom had acquired some Thai lanterns which were released on the town's square during the midnight celebrations. The floating lanterns rose above the town, subsequently prompting letters in the *Harborough Mail* about strange UFO sightings above Market Harborough!

There was much to celebrate because on this day – the last day of the 20th Century – the theatre finally acquired ownership of the shop next door. The planned expansion would take place as soon as funds permitted.

A media campaign was launched to raise the remaining money and fundraising events began in earnest, with the aim of accruing £25,000 a year for the next four years. Grand bazaars, craft fairs, fancy dress bucket collections and theatre open days helped boost the society's coffers.

A garden party was also held at the home of chairman Jan Bass, and actors from the society took to the streets to entertain passers-by with the aim of "grabbing people's attention with costumes", all in the name of bringing the expansion to fruition.

Volunteers had already started work on connecting the theatre to the shop next door, and longest serving member Kate Plowman donned a hard hat to knock out the first brick in the adjoining wall for publicity shots.

The society's then artistic manager Jack Booth touched on the frustrations about the lack of storage space up to this point: "We create scenery, fittings and sometimes even furniture but most items are then painted over or dismantled because we never have storage space. It's the same with props," he said in 2000.

Most of the scenery flats, on which the sets are built, up to now, had been kept on the theatre stage. But the expansion, with the new spaces in the annexe, would aim to rectify this problem – at least in part – and the theatre stage could at last be freed up.

To mark this, some of the theatre's more unusual and memorable props from past shows were exhibited in the newly-opened Green Dragon Room. This was a nice opportunity for some of the theatre's unsung heroes – those stalwarts working behind the scenes – to get their moment in the limelight.

The acquisition of the adjacent shop was a huge and much-welcomed development, thus when the Drama Society entered the new millennium, it did so in fine spirit. That spirit was carried into the first show, literally, with Noel Coward's *Blithe Spirit*.

New actors were arriving thick and fast, Suzy Burgess and Louise Hamilton-Welsh made their debuts.

The vice-chairman of the Citizens Advice Bureau, which had benefited from a gala performance of *Blithe Spirit*, described the theatre, rightly and quite poetically, as "one of the jewels in the crown of our town". This is a message the society continues to spread far and wide.

When the society staged Willy Russell's *Shirley Valentine* – described as one of the most impressive British scripts of the second half of the century – unlike the film version, the play was performed here as a monologue, as it was originally written, with Teresa Kennedy taking on the challenging title role as the bored Liverpudlian housewife.

It was followed by *The Wyrd Sisters* (even though the society admitted most people over 40 would never have heard of the play's author Terry Pratchett at the time), Friel's *Dancing at Lughnasa* (described as a "two-hanky story" and produced by George Kitson who had met the playwright Friel in Belfast some years earlier), Howson's *Staying Here* (forever known as 'sheep play' by members because the cast had to dress as sheep!) and the Bard's *Much Ado About Nothing*, with Kay Carpenter and Ruth Moore.

In a bid to restore the idea of a more formal Gala Night, a special preview performance of *Dancing at Lughnasa* was staged with all the trimmings and some VIP guests, selected through a competition in the local paper. It was a perfect opportunity for theatre-goers to dress up, although it was realised that ball-gowns might be a little too fulsome for theatre seats! "Posh frocks" for ladies and "suits" for chaps was the suggested attire.

Jeanne Moore remembers, with amusement, how choreographer Siobhan Moore (who would at one time star in *Caspar* in the West End) sprung the news that she had to perform an Irish dance for a scene in the play. A 'big ask' considering Jeanne had never before danced on stage!

Staying Here, which took a sideways look at sheep farming and the changing nature of agriculture seemed to have been written for the town. The drama society had agreed to stage the play a year before the foot and mouth crisis swept through the country devastating much of the farming community. It seemed fitting then that collection buckets were passed around the audience after every performance to raise funds for the Addington Fund, to help farmers cope throughout the epidemic.

The play's author Stuart Howson even came to watch a performance on one of the nights and was very impressed, particularly that the society had managed to track down, and use, the same music he had used in his original production.

During rehearsal local undertakers Robin Garfield and David Stamp who were in the play had confessed to practising their lines in one of their hearses (while it was 'unoccupied' obviously!)

In 2001, radical plans to completely demolish the adjoining shop and create a brand new three-storey building, were put in motion. Planning permission was granted, but unfortunately, quotes gained from various construction firms estimated the cost of the project in excess of £800,000.

The trustees, understandably, decided this simply wasn't achievable on the available budget. It was a 'dream too far'.

Undeterred however, it was hoped the expansion could be achieved piecemeal – bit by bit, stage by stage.

Later on, the former Factory Lane ladies' and gentlemen's public toilets, which had been acquired in 2002, were converted, with the help of Carter Design, into the lounge bar we know today. The bar had previously taken up a corner of the lounge and this development freed up vital space for tables and chairs.

As ever, the society's raison d'etre was that the theatre "must be in use", but this certainly wasn't an issue at the time. Over the previous year or so, some fifty organisations had used Harborough Theatre, many of which were not-for-profit bodies. Sixteen used it for theatrical events and over thirty for non-theatre activities, such as coffee mornings and bazaars, etc, in the theatre lounge.

The list of events flagged-up two important things – one, that many were for worthy causes and, two, that quite a few were aimed at children to encourage their interest and involvement in the arts, rather than 'less productive' pursuits!

Bookings, for Saturday morning use of the theatre lounge, were already being taken for the following year and within a week two thirds of available dates had been booked!

Regular activities included Sunday School, Age Concern luncheon club, Roman Way Day Centre café, two bridge clubs, monthly events by the poetry group and an Inland Revenue advice clinic. Other users included Harborough District Council and the Art Club for its annual display of members' work.

The auditorium was also being used as a lecture theatre, and for talks by expert speakers, notably by the Decorative and Fine Art Society, Natural History Society and the Association of Speakers Clubs. Local firms also used the theatre for shareholder meetings.

According to the bookings diary for the coming few months of the new season, there was a window of just two weeks when nothing was happening at Harborough Theatre. It was a case of "squeezing a quart into a pint pot", thus highlighting the desperate need for a theatre redevelopment to enable the building of the "quart pot" that was so necessary.

The excitement of such high activity spilled into the next

productions which included Maugham's *The Constant Wife*, Ayckbourn's festive *Season's Greetings* (which saw the debut of Steve Daniels who would go on to appear on stage many times as well as hosting the occasional theatre quiz night), *The Snowman* presented by youngsters from the Joanne Woodcock School of Dance and Theatre, Miller's masterpiece *Death Of A Salesman* (featuring debuts from Jonathan Brown, Tom Fray, Liz Robertson and Peter Kaye), West End hit *Three Tall Women* (with a debut from Kyle Newman, more well-known for her operatic shows) and restoration comedy *She Stoops To Conquer*.

The season even boasted a 'world premiere' in the shape of *Scherezade's Arabian Nights*, written specifically for the Harborough Theatre stage by local authors Jeremy Thompson and Jane Rowland.

It was during *Death Of A Salesman* that Ruth Moore met future husband Tom Fray. Tom had to portray a character at different stages of life, including as a young boy, while Ruth was playing a 'lady of the night'! Ruth joked that despite this rather unusual introduction, love blossomed and the couple married three years later.

Also in 2002, George Kitson helped bring the brilliant Arts Fresco to Market Harborough which saw around 70 street performers let loose in the town. It became an annual event and continues to be enjoyed by hundreds of people each year. It typified George's philosophy which has always been to, as he puts it, "bring art to the people."

On a sad note, this year saw the death of Arthur Jones, a versatile and talented member who showed great spirit right up until the end. His wife Bunty, also a dedicated society member, died a few months later. A couple of years earlier, the society had lost a great director with the passing of Gordon Henderson and over the coming years it would also mourn the losses of actor Tom Henderson, actress Jean Joule, and Betty Whitelaw, who will always be remembered for her stunning Miss Marple.

In the latter part of 2002, the society would receive one of its greatest ever compliments. One of its performances of *Kindertransport*, which starred Kyle Newman playing the part of a child refugee fleeing Nazi Germany during the war, was attended by a real-life Kinder war child Bertha Leverton. She said the performance "at least equalled or topped the performance in the West End." High praise indeed. Producer Jan Wilson had heard the play on radio, and there had been reservations about adapting it for stage, but the bold move to do it clearly paid off.

The theatre development fund gained a vital boost when the Tudor Players staged romantic comedy *The Kingfisher* in aid of the appeal. Long-standing theatre patrons Godfrey Tabiner and Ian and Queenie Parry took lead roles after a long absence, with Queenie celebrating her fiftieth anniversary as a member of the Tudors Players. Thanks to Ian and Queenie's 'dual citizenship' it was the third time the Tudors had staged a production in aid of the theatre, the first being the Waterhouse-Hall comedy *Say Who You Are* in 1972 and the comedy *Butterflies Are Free* in 1976. This was a fine example of how 'cross pollination' with other theatre groups was benefiting the theatre, both financially and creatively.

The Playboy Of The Western World, which George Kitson produced, featured young society member Drew Webb who would several years later go on to appear on television, notably in the BBC drama *Filth: The Mary Whitehouse Story*, playing Julie Walters' son. George said Drew had shown much potential, having had to master an Irish accent for the role, even though the cast had help from an international voice coach which George had brought in.

In 2003, the theatre scored a real coup when it acquired its first ever patron, the actress Geraldine McEwan.

She had appeared in numerous films such as *Titus, Robin Hood: Prince Of Thieves* and *Henry V* and on television in the *Prime of Miss Jean Brodie* and *The Barchester Chronicles*. She would later, of course, become best known for her role as Miss Marple on television.

Having such a big name attached to the theatre was seen as a great opportunity to raise its profile further. It was a real boon for the drama society at just the right time as still more funds were needed for the redevelopment.

Acquiring a patron was an exciting development as the society rolled into the 2003/04 season, which began rather bravely with a couple of Cowards.

Noel's anachronistic style and wit isn't necessarily for everyone but *Red Peppers* and *Still Life* (filmed as *Brief Encounter*) were delivered assuredly by directors Gill Lucchesi and Brenda Ashburner, respectively.

JB Priestley's fascinating *A Dangerous Corner* returned, described in a review by the Harborough Mail's then news editor Matt Howling, who would later become Publicity Officer for the theatre, as a play "exploring what would happen if we opened the proverbial can of worms…with a denouement that brought gasps from the audience."

Newcomers included Vivien Crowther, Marguerite Hegley, Dennis Henderson and Johanna Ridgley.

Director Anne Hepworth recalled how the play, set in the 1930s, required a radio recording which sounded like the old Home Service. Step forward society stalwart Gerald Heighton who came out of theatre 'retirement' to record the piece for the play. "It was perfect!" Anne said.

Ruth Moore, who also appeared, remembers that a gun which had to be fired during the play had proved unreliable in rehearsals. Poised in the wings during the real performances, however, just in case, was Tom Fray, ready to hit two blocks of wood together to imitate the gunshot. Ruth recalls how one night when the gun actually worked, she swears it was followed the sound of an over-keen Tom thwacking his blocks of wood.

A 'mouthful' of a play arrived in the form of tongue-in-cheek comedy *The Farndale Avenue Housing Estate Townwomen's Guild Dramatic Society's Production Of A Christmas Carol.*

It was a far cry from Ibsen's heavyweight *Hedda Gabler*, which followed and which came with a warning that gunshots will be fired into the audience!

It was a case of life imitating art for the season's final play, Ayckbourn's *A Chorus Of Disapproval* – a 'play within a play' which tells the story of a small market town operatic society trying to find performers for its latest show.

John Foreman who was directing the play recalled that the cast lost its leading man when his company relocated him. "We had to reshuffle parts and then out of the blue, John Tweedie arrived and we had our new 'Guy' at last," John said.

Book store Ottakar's (later Waterstone's) became the theatre's honorary box office, which was ideal due to its central location in the town and the fact it was open seven days a week. (The Harborough District Council offices would take over as the box office a few years later).

No surprise then when tickets sold well for the 2004/05 season's opener *Party Piece*. Trevor Brown, Ian Milner, Dennis Davison and Jack Booth, produced a 'party piece' of their own by building a memorable set depicting two neighbouring terraced houses.

In fact in 2004, Jack Booth and Eileen (nee Bozman) who had met while constructing sets, celebrated their marriage at St Nicholas Church in Little Bowden, attended by many society members. Eileen, who became involved with the theatre in 1999, took over the play-night raffles which continue to swell society funds.

Society member Kevin Quinn, via his bookshop, arranged author nights at the theatre around this time, which proved very popular, attracting such names as Gervaise Phinn, Paul Britton, children's laureate Anne Fine, Clive Aslet, Christopher Matthew, Deric Longden and Michael Wood.

The next play of the season is still considered by many members of the Market Harborough Drama Society to be one of the finest it has ever produced.

Journey's End – a moving depiction of the First World War as seen from the trenches – was staged during Remembrance Week under the direction of George Kitson (who had produced over 100 plays in his life by this time).

R C Sherriff's classic tale of "ordinary men in an extraordinary situation" was based on the playwright's own experience of life in the trenches.

George, a former RAF serviceman himself, had typically carried out meticulous research for the play, even visiting trenches in The Somme in France.

He said: "Going to the trenches was a very moving and evocative experience. Visitors walked around in silence. It was an eerie feeling, like you could imagine the ghosts of the dead soldiers. I wanted to bring a sense of this to the play."

The play's powerful and moving finale in which a shower of poppy petals rain down on motionless soldiers is an image that lives on in the memory. Some members of the audience recall how they remained rooted to their seats even after the curtain had fallen, awe-struck by the power of performance and production.

Fittingly, the gala night raised proceeds for the Royal British Legion.

To complement the performance of *Journey's End*, the moving play *Women of Troy* was staged as an extra-curricular item to the season. It utilised the same set as *Journey's End* and dramatised the stories of those left behind at home during war but those who are not spared the worry, grief and suffering that comes with conflict.

After such highlights, the society came down with a bump when, for only the second time in its 70 year history, it was forced to cancel a run.

Old Tyme Music Hall, due to be staged during the festive season, was cancelled due to illness of members. Cancelling was not a decision the society took lightly.

To compensate, John Foreman pulled out all the stops to schedule a performance of *Same Time Next Year*, which was planned and executed in less than half the normal time.

Another dilemma (creative, this time) was faced with the staging of *Tissue*, a thought-provoking study of a 29-year-old woman (played by Kyle Newman) who finds a lump in her breast.

A play about cancer was always going to be a hard-sell, but the bravery of the drama committee, which selects plays for the season, as well as Jan Wilson in the director's chair, was to be admired.

Despite the predicted small audiences, many of those who saw the play wrote letters to congratulate the drama society on "an outstanding production, with a good set and acting of a high standard."

The play had been particularly moving because Gill Lucchesi (who had been a society member for 20 years and made her final appearance on stage in *Clouds*) had just been diagnosed with cancer. But Gill was keen for *Tissue* to be staged and even advised the cast on such things as the effects of chemotherapy. She died in 2006.

Fittingly, the gala night of *Tissue* provided an opportunity to raise funds for Breakthrough For Breast Cancer.

In 2006, Alan Window's production of Thomas Hardy's *The Day After The Fair* was lauded with awards at the Leicestershire and Rutland Full-Length Play Festival. Alan scooped a gong for best director, Katja Ellis-Mathius and Liz Clarke were joint runners-up in the Best Actress category for their roles as Anna and Edith. And Jessica Monk was runner-up for Best Supporting Actress for her portrayal as Sarah. The production also finished third overall for Best Play.

Alan Window joked that his direction was "better than IVF" as during his run of *The Day After The Fair*, his 'pregnant maid' (Katya) became pregnant for real, and Ruth Fray (nee Moore) became pregnant not long after playing a 'pregnant maid' in *Night Must Fall*, which Alan also directed!

Other highlights included *Hobson's Choice* with Jeanne Moore directing her daughter Ruth in the role of Maggie Hobson, which Jeanne herself had taken in the 1986 version.

Ruth recalled how it had been an honour to appear in it as, not only was it her favourite play of all time, she had worked backstage as a teenager when her mother had appeared in it.

Ruth remembers, with amusement, that during a performance Dave Wortley (playing Hobson) had forgotten to put a vital prop (a writ) in his pocket causing a "moment of panic" on stage. Luckily, Ruth managed to 'ad-lib' her way out of the predicament and saved the day!

Freda Archer retired as president in 2007 after many years serving the society in various capacities. Freda had been a prolific and noted actress in her day, with her favourite stage role being in Terence Rattigan's *The Deep Blue Sea* in 1971.

Freda was known for immersing herself in character for plays, sometimes having her hair cut into period style if the role required!

"The things you do for drama Freda," her colleagues joked.

Freda said recently: "What I remember most is the friendships made and the community spirit. I would love to see this continue."

Queenie Parry took over the role of president from Freda, and Jan Maxwell took over as chairman from Nick Lewis.

Queenie said: "During my term in office, I would love to see the theatre acquire a lift. It would open up the theatre to so many more people."

Aptly, it has recently been announced that the lift project looks set to get the green light after many frustrating years of campaigning.

Queenie also said: "I would also love to see more young people getting involved with the theatre. I think once young people are hooked, they are hooked for life. I know I was!"

In 2008, another momentous milestone was reached when the Drama Society celebrated its 75th anniversary.

To commemorate the landmark, a 75th anniversary committee

was established to plan a series of celebratory events and ensure the year didn't go by unnoticed.

These included a hugely successful open day, a barn dance, carnival float and formal dinner.

This book, *Stage By Stage*, was also brought up to date to mark the anniversary.

More awards were bestowed on the society for plays *The Exorcism* and *The Herbal Bed* (with Mark Bodicoat being named best actor) by the Leicester Drama Federation.

Ongoing redevelopment work has also seen a new fire escape created and the redecoration of the meeting room. Members recently took a vote on whether this room should be christened the Dolphin Suite or the Harlequin Room. On a vote, the latter won.

Also, the cramped wardrobe which had existed for many years underneath the auditorium was moved to a new room in the extension, with everything catalogued and photographed with willing members posing in selected attire! The aim being, according to costume stalwarts Pam Davison and Helen Foreman, to create an easy-to-access brochure of all available costumes for future shows. The old wardrobe space will be used for storage.

So many developments, yet so many aims and ambitions. Even after 75 years, the society refuses to rest on its laurels and, as ever, is looking forward to bigger and better things.

While its past has been shaped by the dedication and efforts of previous or existing society members, what's to come will depend on support from new volunteers. Thus its future remains, to some extent, as unpredictable as many of its great plays. One suspects and hopes however, to paraphrase the showman Al Jolson, "You ain't seen nothing yet…"

Dancing At Lugnasa 2001

Much Ado About Nothing 2001

'Allo 'Allo 2006

The Herbal Bed 2007

Staying Here 2001

Hobson's Choice 2006

Much Ado About Nothing 2001

Constant Wife 2001

Death of a Salesman 2002

Journey's End 2004

Lady's Not for Burning 2005

Kindertransport 2002

Lounge refurbishment 2006

Bar refurbishment 2005

Management Team 1997–2000

Dennis Davison

Jack Booth

Nick Lewis

Geraldine McEwan
Market Harborough Drama Society's Patron since 2003

EPILOGUE

"The applause, delight, the wonder of our stage."
Ben Jonson (1623)

To sum up, the changes and developments over the years have been immense and relentless. At the same time, in its 75th year, the society has not lost sight of its purpose and retained what it does best – its wonderful sense of community and incredible creative output.

Looking back, the sheer variety of plays put on has been quite remarkable.

The enduring beauty of theatre is that the stage can be transformed into any place under the sun, from any time in history.

From the Middle Ages (*The Lady's Not For Burning*), a stately home (*Lettuce and Lovage*), Lancashire in the late 19th Century (*Hobson's Choice*), Nazi-occupied France (*'Allo, 'Allo*) the dusty heat of Andalucia (*Blood Wedding*), a remote Tuscan villa (*God Only Knows*) to the morally-sensitive times of Shakespeare's Stratford Upon Avon (*The Herbal Bed*).

That stage continues to be a platform for the boundless creativity of the drama society and the playwrights whose imaginings it draws upon.

Its patronage has also seen a resurgence. We are not only getting more people through the doors, we are also getting people who have never before ventured into a theatre or seen a play. This can only be welcomed and encouraged.

As Freda Archer's husband Alan put it recently, perhaps the novelty of new technology – television, DVD, the internet, computer games – is wearing off and people are returning to the theatre to see live performance, up close and personal. Hopefully this is true, as nothing quite rivals the theatre for sheer intensity of performance.

One of the amazing things about the drama society is that those with jobs, families and all the other distractions of modern life, continue to find the time to prepare and stage shows to such a high standard, as well as work behind the scenes.

Those treading the boards or helping out backstage, front of house or on committees are to be commended for their tireless devotion.

The voluntary work, carried out by society members during the theatre's many recent redevelopments, has undoubtedly saved tens of thousands of pounds in labour costs. Without their unstinting commitment, the theatre would not be the place it is today.

One undeniable truth is the amount of pleasure the theatre seems to give those involved. There are so many fond memories about past shows (details of which have been preserved in scrapbooks by society archivist Viv Window).

As society member George Kitson put it recently, "It's been a great amorphous of enjoyment". A sentiment no doubt shared by all.

While some members are lost, for whatever reason, the pool of talent continues to be replenished. Although there is always room for more.

It is clear the cultural pull of the theatre, for some, remains irresistible. One suspects also that members are drawn by its sense of community and infectious energy.

What remains at the society's core though, is its strong artistic drive, creative integrity and love of performance.

There is a small section of our audience, we know, which never visits any other theatre but the one in Harborough. This puts welcome pressure on the society to ensure it brings the very best of world theatre to its stage. Also, for every new media-savvy and culturally-savvy patron we entice through the door, we add to the diversity of our audience.

The modern audience is no longer one, homogeneous majority, but rather a range of minorities – people with varying backgrounds, tastes and expectations. This presents a new and exciting challenge.

The society must continue to tap into this diversity and, while always striving to stage sell-outs, never be afraid to challenge its patrons with demanding or unusual material. Never underestimate the audience, and they will never underestimate you.

We are undoubtedly blessed with a wonderful audience. An audience that keeps coming back for more. An audience prepared to see challenging plays, which other theatres have shied away from, and return year after year. It is them who produce the ultimate encore – the audience.

Their loyalty and patronage continues to be awe-inspiring and society members who work so hard to bring plays to the stage, ultimately, remain in their debt.

It is this support, and the dedication of the drama society, that will ensure the theatre continues to take pride of place in the hearts of people in the town and beyond. It is the creative hub of Market Harborough and long may it continue to draw a crowd.

ADDENDUM

The Market Harborough Drama Society would also like to acknowledge the valuable contribution of some other members, who have given their support in years gone by.

These include Maurice Saunders, seen regularly on stage, Howard Biddlestone, a secretary for society in the early days and quite the matinee idol as a leading man, and Hilda Dunkley, who took many leading roles.

The society's first chairman Colin Elliot, who lived in Hillcrest Avenue as well as being the head of a Corby Primary School, and Albert Eads – perhaps the society's first treasurer – and proprietor of Eads Bakery in St Mary's Road, deserve special mention.

Margaret Grey, produced shows in the early years, including Blithe Spirit, and early lighting and sound stalwarts Noel Dyson and George Brawn also gave much of their time. Noel was the local manager for the Kettering Electricity Board and lived above their showroom in Adam and Eve Street, and George had an electrical business in Coventry Road – so they were both handy if anything went wrong.

And, of course, anyone who hasn't been mentioned, but who gave their time over the years so willingly.

PLAY LIST

PRODUCTIONS 1933-1993 in the
Conservative Hall – Liberty Hall – Harborough Theatre
unless shown otherwise.

* = Symingtons' Club Room   @ = Assembly Rooms   # = Cooperative Hall

1933	*Candida	1948-49	They came to a City
1934-35	@Twelfth Night		Busman's Honeymoon
	@Outward Bound		Ladies in Retirement
1935-36	@The Late Christopher Bean		She Passed Through Lorraine
	@An Evening's Entertainment		The Sacred Flame
	@Romeo and Juliet	1949-50	Miranda
1936-37	@Pygmalion		Dr Brent's Household
	@Lady Precious Stream		Alice in Wonderland
	A Dramatic Entertainment		To Kill a Cat
1937-38	@Fortunato, & The Women		The Corn is Green
	Have Their Way	1950-51	Private Lives
	@Juno and The Paycock		The First Mrs Fraser
	#Squaring the Circle		Toad of Toad Hall
1938-39	@Tobias and the Angel		The Linden Tree
	Paradise Enow		A Midsummer Night's Dream
	@Storm in a Teacup	1951-52	While the Sun Shines
	Murder in the Cathedral		The Glass Slipper
1940	The Playboy of the Western		I'll Leave it to You
	World		The Happiest Days of Your Life
	Misalliance		Twelfth Night
1944-45	#The Importance of Being	1952-53	Night Must Fall
	Earnest		Bonaventure
	#Dangerous Corner		Our Town
	#Hands across the Sea		The Ex Mrs Y
	#When We Are Married		The Cure for Love
	#A Murder Has Been Arranged	1953-54	The Merchant of Venice
1945-46	#The Dragon and the Dove, &		The Importance of Being Earnest
	A Change for the Worse		The White Sheep of the Family
	*The magistrate		Gaslight
	#Blithe Spirit	1954-55	Tovarich
1946-47	#Maria Marten		Cranford
	*The light of Heart		Maiden Ladies
1947-48	The Two Mrs Carrolls		Corinth House
	Mr Pym Passes By		The Druid's Rest
	I Have Been Here Before	1955-56	As You Like It
	Hay Fever		The Happy Marriage
	Grand National Night		Beauty and the Beast
	It Depends What You Mean		Peg o' my Heart

1956-57	On Monday Next		September Tide
	A Cradle of Willow		The Amorous Prawn
	Mad About Men	1965-66	All for Mary
	A Question of Fact		Night Must Fall
1957-58	Macbeth		Post-Horn Gallop
	The Holly and the Ivy		An Ideal Husband
	Mary Rose		Photo Finish
	Man about the House		This Thing Called Love
	The Love Match		(The Carl Clifford Puppet
1958-59	My Three Angels		Theatre, Northampton)
	Plaintiff in a Pretty Hat	1966-67	Goodnight Mrs Puffin
	Dr Morelle		A Letter from the General
	The Late Christopher Bean		Pygmalion
1959-60	The Isle of Umbrellas		Cinderella
	Sailor Beware		Midsummer Mink
	The Taming of the Shrew		Murder on the Nile
	The Whole Truth	1967-68	Waltz of the Toreadors
	Antigone		Fool's Paradise
1960-61	Dial M for Murder		The Winter's Tale
	Under Milk Wood		Music Hall
	The Noble Spaniard		The Grass is Greener
	Nude With Violin		A Horse! A Horse!
	Gigi		Waiting in the Wings
1961-62	Wild Goose Chase	1968-69	Romanoff and Juliet
	Rope		The Reluctant Debutante
	The Tempest		Gaslight
	Breath of Spring		Private Lives
	(at Little Bowden Hall)		The Shop at Sly Corner
	Doctor in the House	1969-70	Separate Tables
1962-63	The Sound of Murder		Murder at the Vicarage
	Haul for the Shore		The Love Match
	Book of the Month		My Three Angels
	The Rape of the Belt		Billy Liar
	The Caretaker		Relatively Speaking
	Not in the Book		Tonight at 8.30 (Red Peppers,
	Sabrina Fair		Hands Across the Sea, Still Life)
	Nuts in July		Anything Can Happen (Youth
	Holiday for Simon		Theatre)
	(Sibbertoft Players)	1970-71	Bell, Book and Candle
1963-64	The Lady's Not for Burning		Spring and Port Wine
	See How They Run		Harvey
	Othello		Cinderella
	Trial and Error		Tom Jones
	Look Back in Anger		The Deep Blue Sea
	The Girl Who Couldn't Quite	1971-72	Conkers, a revue
	Arsenic and Old Lace		The Private Ear & The Public Eye
1964-65	Blithe Spirit		Ten Little Niggers
	Hamlet		Jack and the Beanstalk
	A Midsummer Night's Dream		The Chalk Garden
	The Two Faces of Murder		The Chiltern Hundreds
	The Bride and the Bachelor		Say Who You Are (Tudor Players)

1972-73	Celebration	(EMMA Theatre Company)
	Oh! What a Lovely War!	1979-80	Angels in Love
	The Heartless Princess		The Aspern Papers
	The House on the Cliff		Toad of Toad Hall
	Sweeney Todd		Dear Brutus
	The Mayor of Torontal		Night Watch
1973-74	Pools Paradise		The Importance of Being Earnest
	The Prime of Miss Jean Brodie	1980-81	A Talk in the Park, & Gosforth's
	A Christmas Carol		Fete (at The Woodlands)
	Old Time Music Hall		The Conjur'd Spirit
	The Summer of the Seventeenth		Murder in the Cathedral
	Doll		(in St Dionysius Church)
	The Unexpected Guest		The Lover
1974-75	When We Are Married		The Rose and Crown, & Still Life
	Hay Fever		Triple Bill: The Stronger,
	Dick Whittington		Pastiche, & The Bespoke
	(at Welland Park College)		Overcoat
	Ghosts		Round and Round the Garden
	The Secretary Bird		(at East Langton Grange)
	Roots	1981-82	Hotel Paradiso
	The Ghost Train		Cinderella
1975-76	Boeing-Boeing		Triple Bill: A Shocking Accident,
	The Day After the Fair		Mortmain, & The Dock Brief
	Busy Body		The Crucible
	Salad Days		The Hollow
	Plaza Suite		The Entertainer
	Lady Windermere's Fan		Operatic Selection (Opera
	Salad Days, repeated		Minima)
	Butterflies Are Free (Tudor		The Mummers' Play
	Players)		(round the villages)
1976-77	Alfie		Ten of the Best (Couronne Ballet)
	Come Closer Now		The Snow Queen (Leics Youth
	Arms and the Man		Theatre)
	The Two of Us	1982-83	Table Manners
	Love is..		Was He Anyone?
	The Boy Friend		(Robert Smyth Youth Theatre)
	The Lark		Dangerous Corner
1977-78	The Happy Apple		Aladdin
	Not Now, Darling		Wild Goose Chase
	The Holly and the Ivy		Rattle of a Simple Man
	A Man for All Seasons		(Northampton Royal Theatre)
	Huis Clos		The Glass Menagerie
	View from the Bridge		Virtue in Danger
	Rookery Nook		A Taste of Honey
1978-79	Murder with Love		(Leicester Phoenix)
	Halfway Up the Tree	1983-84	(Jubilee season)
	John Willie and the Beeple		Living Together
	Candida		The Killing of Sister George
	Wedding of the Year		Corinth House
	Tartuffe		Fifty Years of Golden Musicals
	The Great Little Tilley		The Constant Wife

Hamlet
Rosencrantz and Guildestern Are
Dead
Relative Values
(Hopscotch Theatre Company)

1984-85 The Sound of Murder
Present Laughter
Dick Whittington
The Twelve-Pound Look, &
The Laboratory
Habeas Corpus
Our Town
The Late Late Christmas Carol
(Derby Playhouse Company)
Footloose and Fancy Free
(Couronne Ballet)

1985-86 Richard III
(at Bosworth Field)
Abigail's Party
The Old Lady Shows Her
Medals, & A Civil Marriage
Babes in the Wood
Lady Chatterley's Lover
(Derby Playhouse Company)
Outside Edge
A Talent to Influence
(London Connection Company)
Hobson's Choice
The Gioconda Smile

1986-87 Twelfth Night
All In Good Time
The Wizard of Oz
Relatively Speaking
The Dear Departed, & Half an
Hour
Murder Mistaken
See How They Run

1987-88 She Stoops To Conquer
Whose Life Is It Anyway?
Snow White
Old Time Music Hall
A Murder Is Announced
What Every Woman Knows
A Fish Out Of Water
Cowardy Custard
Let's Face The Music
(Couronne Ballet)

1988-89 How The Other Half Loves
Pack of Lies
Puss in Boots
Farewell, Farewell Eugene

On Golden Pond
A Variety Evening
Lord Arthur Savile's Crime

1989-90 When We Are Married
Rebecca
Cinderella
The Farndale Avenue Housing
Estate Townswomen's Guild
Dramatic Society Production of
Macbeth
Betrayal
The Merchant of Venice

1990-91 Old Time Music Hall
84 Charing Cross Road
A Fishy Business, & The Will
Peter Pan
Absent Friends
Beyond Reasonable Doubt
Blithe Spirit

1991-92 Under Milk Wood
Drinking Companions, &
A Talk in the Park
Dangerous Obsession
Mother Goose
Oh! What a Love War!
Happy Days
The Widowing of Mrs Holroyd
The Farmer's Wife

1992-93 Maud (Valentine Pelka, R S C)
Waiting in the Wings
The Exorcism
Aladdin
The Old Curiosity Shop
(Northampton Royal Company)
Bedroom Farce
Gaslight
Rookery Nook
The Rose and Crown, & Still Life

1993/4 Diamond Jubilee Year
Candida
The Winter's Tale
Beauty And the Beast
The Happiest Days of Your Life
Murder at the Vicarage
The Importance Of Being Earnest

1994/95 My Mother Said I Never Should
The Business of Murder
Dick Whittington
The Lion in Winter
Henceforward
The Boyfriend

1995/96	Noises Off	Scherezade's Arabian Nights
	The Diary of Ann Frank	Death of a Salesman
	Toad of Toad Hall	Three Tall Women
	The Last of the Red Hot Lovers	She Stoops to Conquer
	Antigone	2002/2003 When We Are Married
	The Physicist	Kindertransport
	Daisy pulls It Off	The Boy who Fell into a Book
1996/97	A Midsummer Night's Dream	Death Trap
	Talking Heads (a Lady of Letters,	The Kingfisher (Tudor Players)
	Soldiering On, A Woman of No	Shakers
	Importance)	The Playboy Of the Western
	Winners	World
	Jack And the Beanstalk	2003/2004 An Evening with Noel Coward
	All My Sons	Red Peppers
	Teechers	Still Life
	Cat's Cradle	Dangerous Corner
	Fighting Chance	The Farndale Avenue Housing
1997/98	Double Cut	Estate Townswomen's Guild
	Educating Rita	Dramatic Society's production of
	Zigger Zagger	A Christmas Carol
	A Christmas Carol	Hedda Gabbler
	The Woman Who Cooked Her	Clouds
	Husband	A Chorus of Disapproval
	Touched	2004/2005 Party Piece
	The Writing Game	Journey's End
	Old Time Music Hall	Old Time Music Hall (cancelled)
1998/99	Sailor Beware	Tissue
	Separate Tables	The Cemetery Club
	The Lion the Witch and the	The Lady's Not For Burning
	Wardrobe	Same Time Next Year
	Talking Heads (A Cream Cracker	2005/2006 Shadowlands
	Under the Settee, A Chip in the	Veronica's Room
	Sugar, Bed among the Lentils)	Lettuce and Lovage
	Verdict	Hobson's Choice
	Good Companions	The Day After the Fair
1999/2000	Fish Out of Water	'Allo 'Allo
	An Inspector Calls	2006/2007 Time Of My Life
	The Railway Children	Blood Wedding
	Death and the Maiden	Night Must Fall
	Shakespeare at the Green Dragon	God Only Knows
	Happy Families	Quartet
2000/2001	Blithe Spirit	Amy's View
	Shirley Valentine	2007/2008 The Herbal Bed
	The Wyrd Sisters	The Heiress
	Dancing at Lugnasa	Arsenic and Old Lace
	Staying Here	The Exorcism
	Much Ado About Nothing	Blue Remembered Hills
2001/2002	The Constant Wife	See How They Run
	Season's Greetings